My Best Advice

Letters To...
Our Teenage Sons

by
Michael Kenneth Chapman

Edited by
Two Time Emmy Nominee
Margaret Ford-Taylor

**My Best Advice
Letters To...
Our Teenage Sons**

**Michael K. Chapman
Co-Author**

DEDICATION

I dedicate this book…

…To my wonderful mother Pastor Eloise C. Corbin, for always encouraging me and teaching me the importance of faith and the power of prayer. Thanks *"momma"* for all the sacrifices you have made so I can live my dreams. With all my heart…I love you!

…In loving memory of my *"Big-sister"* **Debra Marie Chapman**…You will always be missed.

How To Use This Empowerment Tool Book

1st. READ your daily empowerment letter based on the *date* of your current calendar.

2nd. WRITE in your journal a new thought or idea immediately. Also, read page 151 on how to set and achieve your goals.

3rd. SPEAK out loud your *"I-Promise"* affirmations twice daily (morning & afternoon), see page 4.

ENJOY! ENJOY! ENJOY!

This Book Is
Exclusively For

_____

From _____

_____

_____

_____

_____

_____

_____

"I Promise"

- **I promise** I will not make EXCUSES...but make adjustments.

- **I promise** I will RESPECT myself, my peers, my teachers and all adults in and out of school.

- **I promise** I will be prepared for school every day because that is MY RESPONSIBILITY.

- **I promise** I will complete all my school assignments on time and seek assistance immediately as I need it.

- **I promise** I will go to school EVERY DAY and maintain a positive attitude...ALL DAY.

- **I promise** I will VALUE my EDUCATION by placing it so HIGH that nothing comes before it...ABSOLUTELY NOTHING!

- **I promise** I will read this DECLARATION AND MY GOALS twice a day!

- **I promise** I will say to myself, *"If I fail at any or all of these endeavors, I will forgive myself and try even harder tomorrow!"*

INTRODUCTION

Introduction. I read where billionaire entrepreneur Oprah Winfrey once said *"even the wildest dreams have to start somewhere. Allow yourself the time and space to let your mind wonder and your imagination to fly."* With that said, you hold in your hands a book that was written from an idea, but mostly from the heart of 31-positive men from across the U.S. From the onset I must inform you that this book is not intended as a one-stop to solve all your life's issues. However, if you wish to change your life for the better, build stronger relationships, learn to set and achieve your goals, learn some new skills and new ideas about self-respect, self-esteem and self-confidence, then, in your hands, you have a road map, a blue print that will help you to BEGIN to structure or restructure your life and your future. An ancient African Proverb says…*"It takes a village to raise a child."* Consider this book the collective thoughts and advice gathered from within that village. This empowerment tool book has been thoughtfully put together with young men in mind; because we know we are obligated to do everything in our power to ensure that our sons (*and daughters*) become vibrant and contributing members of society.

Let me share a story that demonstrates the power of an idea coupled with persistence. It concerns the birth and creation of this book series.

Inception. From the time my God-daughter Mariah (whom I affectionately call "Precious") was 14 years of age I would hand write and mail her an encouragement letter every other month. Though she lives less than 10 miles away I thought it was "cool" for her to receive a letter in the mail in the midst of all the bills and junk mail mom was receiving. My purpose was to encourage her to do well in school; i.e. to respect herself, her peers and adults, and to place a high value on her education so that nothing could touch it. I was keenly aware that the second half of her sophomore year she would be facing the infamous five-part Ohio Graduation Test (OGT). Before testing time came I restructured the letters with a new purpose in mind because I wanted to do all I could to increase herself-confidence for the test. One of the methods I initiated was the power of "self-talk." I designed a declaration entitled **"I-Promise"** and she was to read it aloud in the morning, before lunch and before bed time. There is one included in this book as well…and just as powerful. OGT testing time came and by the grace of God, tutoring, and hard work Mariah, passed all five parts on her first try.

Two years quickly went by and she was a senior set to graduate in June of 2010 from Shaw High School in East Cleveland, Ohio. One day, as I was giving some thought to a creative graduation gift, I had what I considered to be an ingenious idea!

The Power of an Idea. That idea was to petition 31-women to write a letter about the ups and downs of life after high school. I would get the letters edited, put them in a binder, title it and present it to my God-daughter as a book entitled, *"My Best Advice: Letters To...My Graduating Daughter."* Unfortunately, time ran out. Cash is always a good trump-card, so I played my hand and made a cash gift at graduation time instead. However, the idea of 31-letters in book form never died. In early August of the same year, and after conversations with several friends I decided to take on the challenge of putting my idea into book form. The first thing I did was to research teen topics and issues and that is how I chose the 12 hot topics found in this book. Next, I asked 31 women to pick a topic to write about. Finally, I pitched my idea to Miss Ford-Taylor (see About Editor), to see if she would edit the 31-letters. Unequivocally, she said YES!

Finally. From August 2010 through May 2012 I worked diligently to complete this book project. The journey was interesting to say the least. I can recall several times when I almost threw in the towel even though I believed passionately in the project and what I was doing. My intent was to keep my goals in front of me and not to lose focus. I admit I was driven. As a matter of fact, some people became a little annoyed because all I would talk about was *"the book."* I remember one particularly discouraging period when the project stalled as I waited for responses from contributors. At first, I panicked. And then I got angry. I knew this was a wonderful, worthwhile project. Why wasn't it moving? Finally, I stood flat-footed in front of the mirror with tears streaming down my face and said *"Michael, come hell or high water you're not quitting no matter what happens or how long it takes."* I told myself that *"greater is He who is in me than he who is in the world."* By the way, I had to visit the mirror several times on the journey, but I was determined not to quit.

To be honest, I had dropped the ball other times in my past and this time I was committed to go all the way. Plus, something inside would not let me quit. Shortly after the first "reckoning," I received an e-mail with a letter attached to it. The following month I received another e-mail and it was a powerful letter as well.

Then the thought came to me, what better way was there of getting in touch with and engaging dynamic, caring women who would keep the ball rolling than through women who had those same traits? So, to keep the momentum going, I asked the selected women not only to contribute but also for as many referrals as they could give me. As you can see, it worked. The evidence is in your hands. So, read, read, read, use and enjoy. I sincerely believe there is something *life-giving* in this book for everyone.

Please Note: The success formula applied for the conception of the girl's book was used for the creation of the boy's book you have in your hands. So, read, read, read use and enjoy!

Michael K. Chapman
Co-Author

CONTENTS

Part One

31-Empowerment Letters & Journal

11

Part Two

"What a lot we lost when we stopped
writing letters. You can't
re-read a phone call."

-Liz Carpenter

PART ONE

31-Empowerment Letters

&

Private Journal

Empowerment Day 1

By Mark L. Washington
Edited by Margaret Ford-Taylor

Bullying

Greetings,

My best advice today concerns bullying. A person should never, ever let themselves get so distracted that they allow someone else to take control of their personal space. That's what the bully does. He controls a personal space that is not his own. It is a sickness that, at first, only the bully needs to address but it's important to know that the bully could not function without a victim and the victim is also sick if he continues to allow himself to be bullied. To stop this relentless cycle, the victim must learn to say "no" and mean it. No one has the right to invade and control someone else's personal space but it can only be done with permission. It is not only the victim's right to control his or her personal space, it is also his or her responsibility. That is what I want you to understand today. If the bully functions, it's because the victim allows him to.

The bully is a loser and a coward. Why would anyone relinquish their personal space, their life, to a loser and a coward? The bully is, also, obviously out of control of his own life and circumstances. That's why they need to meddle in someone else's. The victim must begin to recognize this and say "no." The victim must decide to mentally, physically, emotionally and/or spiritually remove himself from the place the bully inhabits. One doesn't *have* to participate in whatever sick games the bully invents in order to dominate. Don't hesitant about taking a responsible adult into your confidence. Seeking ways to eliminate the bully from your personal space in order to take and keep charge of one's life is actually smart because when there are consequences to be paid, the bully will be nowhere in sight. Actually, because they are cowards, when actually confronted, most bullies will actually slither away. Strength and resolve scares them and they go to look for the weaknesses they thrive on. Don't let that be you. Bolster your self-esteem to the point that you know your worthiness. Something negative in their life has turned them into the person they are. That's not your concern. Stay plugged into your studies, the positive friends and activities in your life and never bow down to the bully. Ridicule is a common tool of the bully. Remember, it's just a tool to take you down. It doesn't actually mean that what they are saying or doing is funny or real or cool.

17

It means they have discovered a way to make you feel insecure and vulnerable. Your obvious hurt is the reward. Don't give them the satisfaction. As a matter of fact, don't waste time addressing the insult. Square your shoulders look them straight in the eye without blinking and say, *"Something is very wrong with you. You should really get professional help"* and mean it. Once the bully realizes you recognize them for the sick person they actually are and that you are going to stand up to them with confidence, *their* defenses begin to crumble. It's *your* life and *your* personal space. Take charge of it *TODAY* and remember as President Franklin D. Roosevelt once stated, *"You have nothing to fear but fear itself."*

Have a great day!

Day 1 Journal

_____

_____

_____

_____

_____

_____

_____

_____

_____

_____

Empowerment Day 2

By Andrew Howard
Edited by Margaret Ford-Taylor

Dating

Greetings,

Today my best advice concerns dating; It doesn't matter if it is an informal date such as ending up at the same event accidently and then pairing off or a formal situation that has been planned for some time complete with suits and rented cars, the initial advice is the same. Personal hygiene, including deodorant, teeth and fingernails is the front forerunner. In the case of planned dates, be on time. It's only courteous. Details regarding the day or evening should have been worked out between the two of you in advance.

Next comes the most challenging part of the equation. Why are you dating? Hopefully, it's not for negative reasons such as trying to impress friends or planning to take negative advantage of someone. Is it a relationship with a friend that has taken a more serious turn? Advice that is applicable to any kind of dating should be applied here. Be kind, be courteous and be careful. It may make you nervous at first because there is a difference in the relationship but dating a friend is the best and easiest of options. She knows you and you know her. You should eventually be able to relax and enjoy what you two have planned to do. On the other hand, is it someone you don't know well but genuinely like and want to impress? What is the plan? My advice to you is don't overspend, overdress or over talk. Be yourself. She already likes you well enough to go on a date with you so you're ahead of the game. Above all, be courteous. Ask her questions about herself, her family and her interests. Each answer can be followed up with corresponding conversation about *you, your* family and *your* interests. The first step in is to become friends. Get to know each other. By this time in your life you should have some ideas and opinion about what's going on in the world. Introduce subjects but don't dwell on them. The million-dollar tip of the day is learn to listen and listen to learn. Be smart enough to pick up clues from her in terms of how well the date is going. Follow her lead as long as it is not headed toward something that's a negative for you but be prepared to pick up the ball and run with it if necessary. It's still a man's thing. The idea of sex may enter the atmosphere at some point. My advice to you is to steer away from it. It's natural but it's hormonal and control of yourself and your body is in *your* hands. It has very little to do with actual love. To love is to be responsible.

I repeat, it's your animal hormones acting up. Control yourself and think about that cold shower you're going to take when you get home. Don't entertain the notion that such thoughts are new and/or different. They're not. They are as old as life itself but if you're old enough to date, you're old enough to be responsible. If you have a sister or girl cousin, think of how you would want them to be considered, treated, respected and protected on a date. If you don't have any of those females in your family, think of your mother. She's a grown up girl. Think about the nice, long life you are planning for yourself. It may or may not include the person you are out with. Enjoy the date. Try to make certain she enjoys the date. Then take her home and live to repeat the experience if you both decide to. In the meantime, happy dating!

Have a great day!

Day 2 Journal

EMPOWERMENT DAY 3

By Daniel Hill
Edited by Margaret Ford-Taylor

Suicide

Greetings,

My advice to you, today, concerns suicide. I am very happy that you are reading this but I hope it is just for information and research. I hope that you know that suicide is not an option for *you* for many, many reasons. Many people consider suicide because they are so depressed about life that they think they want to leave it. Perhaps you can be of help to someone by letting them know how important living and life are. The teenager who considers suicide should know that as long as it is a thought it can be stopped. The person who actually commits suicide is just feeling, *not thinking. Feelings are important but right now it's time to stop feeling and start thinking.* The person who commits suicide is not thinking about a lot of things. They're not thinking about the vacuum they will leave if they actually carry out the feelings that brought them to this point.

I wonder if they have thought about the wonderful children they would have had one day who would have looked just like them and what a special one-of-a-kind parent they would have been? *I wonder* if they thought about the spectacular kind of person they would have matured into and the contributions that only they were created to make happen? *I wonder* if they considered the person they would have married and who will now miss knowing how very special a mate he or she was? *I wonder* if they thought about all the holidays and birthdays and anniversaries contained in a life time and that they will now miss? *I wonder* if they gave a thought to the stories and dreams and hopes and aspirations they would have been a part of but now, won't? *I wonder* if they ever considered that whatever the problem is right now, it won't be there forever and how long forever is? Have they considered that all feelings are temporary and as unhappy as they are today they can plan to be equally as happy tomorrow if they are here for those of us who care to work on the problem. And there are so many of us who do care but won't have a chance to show it if in a despondent moment or moments a person decides to leave and never come back. Because that is what death is, a forever state. Death is vicious and ugly and does not care about those it destroys.

On the other hand, there are live people who *do* care, many of whom, as a teenager, you haven't even met yet. Plan to stick around and meet them. Give them and life a chance.

I promise you, you won't regret it Suicide is *not* an option. Life is. A wise person once said, ***life is what you make it. Okay, let's go then***. Reach deep down deep and find the courage and the hope and the promise that I know lives there inside you, to want to live. Let the people who love you know that life has gotten just a little bit heavy and you need them. You may be surprised at how many of us there are. *Suicide is not an option. Life is, so let's get on with it!* Close your eyes for a moment and imagine yourself in a warm circle of light and love and those who care about you. We're here! So just for now, plan to have a glorious and wonderful day!

Have a great day!

National Suicide Prevention Lifeline
1-800-273-8255
<u>Available 24 hours EVERYDAY!</u>

May God Continue To Bless Your Life!

Day 3 Journal

_____

_____

_____

_____

_____

_____

_____

_____

_____

Empowerment Day 4

By Dennis Jefferies
Edited by Margaret Ford-Taylor

Fatherhood

Greetings,

My best advice for you today concerns fatherhood. Once, I heard a friend of mine who had become very successful himself but who was, originally, from a very low-income family say, "I know how to be a father because I had one" which I found to be a pretty powerful statement because I saw it as a salute to the millions of fathers in the world who set positive examples for their sons and grandsons, daily, regardless of their economic situation. The history of Black fathers in America is troubling due, first, to the institution of slavery and, next, to the social destruction of the past 50 years as advanced by the drug epidemic and the introduction of new technologies. Through it all, the role of fathers, like the role of mothers, has continually adjusted and readjusted itself to accommodate changing and shifting mores. In the great American play, <u>Fences</u>, by August Wilson, the father goes on a rant bellowing to his teenage son that as a father it was his duty to take care of his son (as in feed, clothe and provide housing) not to *like* him (as in *love*). Not so. Whether it has been serviced or not, one factor remains steadily and unchangingly consistent and that is the need of the boy child for the love, example and guidance of a male figure, preferably, a father. This is not to say the girl child does not have corresponding needs. She does, most emphatically, but the male child's needs are different because he is a male just as you are. Providing the everyday essentials of living is automatically included in the three essentials I noted, the greatest of which is love in the case of both the male and female child. Love is shown in a myriad of tangible ways including providing food and shelter. This has not always been possible for the African American male. Fortunately, what's most important in making love the priority it should be, is to be there, to be present in a child's life. This is possible for you. As a teenager, it is possible for you to begin to plan your life so that you can "be there" for your son as well as your daughter and also provide, or help to provide, the everyday living essentials as you guide them from childhood into adulthood. Fatherhood is a presence that should be felt as much as possible. That is just one of the many reasons why it is so important that you *think* before you participate in unprotected sex. You want to be ready to raise and support a child. You want to be able to give your child the best of life and of you.

You want to be a *married/adult*. If you do, inadvertently, become a parent, it is critical, as a parent, that your presence becomes a part of the child's growing up. Make it a part. Read about fatherhood. Look it up on the internet. Look around you for positive everyday examples of positive role models. Develop a moral code yourself that you can pass on to your child by example. Do as much as you can to help with everyday living expenses but failing everything else, be there. Make your presence felt. Walks with your child during the different seasons does not cost money. A phone call to express your love, visits to the child's school, cards on special days and notes in between involve minimum cost but they say you care. They say that you are there. Above all, talk to your child and let him or her know, without fail, that they have their father's love and that you are there for them always as I am for you.

Have a great day!

Day 4 Journal

_____

_____

_____

_____

_____

_____

_____

_____

_____

_____

EMPOWERMENT DAY 5

By Eli Scott
Edited by Margaret Ford-Taylor

Money

Dear Son

My best advice for you today concerns money and it begins with, "Do not let the word HUSTLE frighten you." To hustle simply means, *"to act upon the desire and willingness to make something happen for one's self."* Some of the world's greatest inventors and richest individuals became successful because of this willingness to hustle. So don't let it frighten you. Just look at it in a positive light because when I talk about hustling, I do not mean selling drugs or stolen merchandise or anything else that's wrong, legally or morally. That would just be stupid. I mean having a mindset that includes being open to traditional and non-traditional ways of making money, that is, knowing that **when you can solve problems for people you don't ever have to be broke**. My dentist solves teeth problems. My barber solves hair problems. My plumber solves plumbing problems and so on. Hopefully, one day when you have completed your education you will be able to solve greater more specialized problems for people.

32

In the meantime your skills are limited because you are still learning but in the meantime, what problems can you solve for others that will give you dollars to spend and/or save? **Make a list and here's a start: Pet sitting. Babysitting. Tutoring younger kids. Shoveling snow or cutting lawns. D.J. for kids' parties. Running errands for neighbors.** The list is endless if you're creative, not lazy and not afraid to hustle. The next thing is to create a really great card and/or flyer to be passed out to neighbors, relatives and friends. On the flyer, include endorsements from professional people who know you. Once you get started, add endorsements from satisfied customers. Check out your personal appearance including your breath before you leave home and then show up for the job ON TIME. Don't be afraid to help some elderly or disabled person for whatever they can spare. It never hurts to be kind and considerate. You actually can't lose *but* it may result in a bigger tip than you'd bargained for. But this is about money so your standard fee should be just *under* minimum wage. If the person could afford more they would probably call in a professional. Don't be greedy. **Hustle**. And don't worry about what you think the person could actually afford to pay. That's not your concern and it will only make you sour and bitter.

Value every penny you earn. Your time will come. Next, don't do a good job. Do an **excellent** job. Don't be afraid to work. Hard work never hurt anybody and your clients will be impressed, I promise you. They'll tell others and your list will grow. Keep the list with phone numbers, updated. Be courteous and remember, "Yes and no, Sir" and "Yes and no, Mam" will *always* works to your advantage. If you haven't heard from someone for a few weeks, pick a Saturday and call to just say "hi" and to make certain there isn't something you can do for them.

Once you start to earn money, value it. Set aside a certain amount for saving and don't touch it. Watch it grow. There will *always* be things to buy. Be picky and choosy about what you spend your hard-earned money on. But always, always maintain a savings account. Begin to think about how you can make your money work for you and not for somebody else. So, I hope you find some helpful advice in this letter. You can always expand it by looking up money making advice on the internet. In the meantime, plan your work and work your plan!

Have a wonderful day.

Day 5 Journal

_____

_____

_____

_____

_____

_____

_____

_____

_____

_____

_____

EMPOWERMENT DAY 6

By Joey Patrick
Edited by Margaret Ford-Taylor

Bullying

Greetings,

My best advice today concerns bullying. I recently read a startling statistic that stated over 3.2 million students are victims of bullying each year. In too many cases, the person being bullied cannot figure out how to correct the situation and so they lead miserable day-to-day lives, sometimes for years. There have been too many cases where suicide was thought to be the answer. It is not and never will be. First of all, look at that statistic. 3.2 million students. So if you are having a problem with a bully, first know that you are not alone even though too often it feels as if you are. Secondly, no one has the right to make your life miserable even for one minute of the day. Know this and plan to do something about it. Please listen. It's alright to tell. Bullying is wrong, cowardly and against the law. So seek counsel. Don't be afraid or ashamed. Wanting to hide it is the child in you. The adult in you knows that you are on the road to manhood and someone is standing in your way.

Remove them by getting help. If you are being bullied physically, it's time to involve your parents, the school counselor and maybe even the police. You are not being less manly if it is a physical bully. You are being smart. Don't get engaged in a battle you know you are going to lose. That's *not* smart. You will definitely win when you show the bully that you will stand up for yourself and that you will turn him over to the proper authorities whose job it is to deal with bullies and other cowards and criminals. If it's not a physical situation, your response is the same in that you refuse to be bullied. If someone bullies you in ways that are not physical, it's just as critical but needs to be handled in a different way.

First of all, let's look at the definition of a bully. A bully is someone who is insecure mentally, physically or emotionally or perhaps a combination of the three. Something in the bully's life has made him or her feel "less than." The bully is a coward. Whatever that "something" is makes the bully afraid most or all of the time. There's nothing abnormal about being afraid. It's how your fear causes you to act that decides whether you are a coward or not. The bully is a coward because instead of working to conquer the fear, he/she decides to compensate by trying to make someone else feel "less than".

Because the bully is an insecure coward, he/she has a need to punish someone, anyone. And, again, because the bully is an insecure coward, he/she looks around for the most weakest, most vulnerable, most susceptible victim they can attack. Don't let that be you. You don't have to be weak mentally, physically nor emotionally. If you have trouble in any of those areas, work on them. Strengthen yourself. Work on being the best you you can be. You can be sensitive, kind and caring without being vulnerable. When I say "vulnerable" I mean you don't have to think of and treat those attributes as weaknesses. Someone, especially bullies will try to convince you that they are. Know that they are not. Know that they are strengths that add to your value as a person. You don't have to be susceptible to another person's insecurities and cruelties because those are his or her problems, not yours. Stop them in their tracks. Let them know that you think too much of yourself to be a scapegoat for their problems. Don't make excuses for who and what you are. Everyone has to work at being better if they want to be better so if you have some areas about yourself that concern you, work on them but don't think that makes you less than anybody. Make that your decision.

Not somebody else's. You are you and you need to think, feel, *know* that that's pretty wonderful-because it is. So, before you leave home in the morning, look in the mirror and say, ***"Stay in your own lane Bully, because, for today, this one is mine."***

Have a great day!

Day 6 Journal

_____

_____

_____

_____

_____

_____

_____

_____

_____

EMPOWERMENT DAY 7

By Sean Miller
Edited by Margaret Ford-Taylor

Healthy Hygiene

Greetings,

My best advice today concerns healthy hygiene. This is one of the simpler topics you will find in this book but it is vitally important that you take today's advice. A few years ago, an adult was responsible for keeping you clean. You're approaching manhood and beginning to make decisions for yourself so having healthy hygiene is now your responsibility. Please take it seriously. Don't wait for some embarrassing moment when someone at school comments or someone in a crowd moves away from you. It's simple. Wash, wash, wash. Bathe or shower at least once a day using hot water and a good strong soap. If you are physically active make that twice a day. Pay particular attention to those areas where hair grows and those that are not open such as between your toes. Buy a small brush from the dollar store and clean your fingernails at least once a day. Cut your fingernails at least once a week. They will look neater and will be much easier to keep clean. Pick out a good strong deodorant and use it each time *after* you wash.

Never, *never* apply deodorant until you have washed thoroughly. And that's not an end to the washing. Wash your hands with soap and hot water *every time* you use the bathroom. Always dry with a clean towel. As a part of your healthy hygiene routine, brush your teeth and floss at least twice a day, once in the morning and just before going to bed. Don't rush. Brush thoroughly including your tongue which carries a lot of bacteria. If you eat strong foods such as onions and garlic, find a midday time to add an additional brushing. Use a mouth wash such as Listerine to help keep your mouth and teeth healthy and your breathe fresh. Annual dental checkups should help avoid bad breath by catching any teeth that may be going bad and also by providing a good strong professional teeth cleaning. Brushing bad teeth won't keep odor away because bad teeth are a sign of infection. Let a dentist help you take care of your teeth for cosmetic as well as health reasons. Also as a part of your healthy hygiene routine, make certain your clothes are clean. Dirty clothes on a clean body won't work.

You're old enough to wash a couple of loads of clothes on Saturday morning. So make a plan and do so.

Make it a habit to wear clean clothes when you leave home including sox and underwear.

The beginning of a healthy body is a clean body. So map out that personal healthy hygiene plan and begin using it today. You may be surprised at how much better you will feel about yourself and the world around you.

Have a great day!

Day 7 Journal

_____

_____

_____

_____

_____

_____

_____

_____

_____

_____

Empowerment Day 8

By Louis J. Green
Edited by Margaret Ford-Taylor

Abuse

Greetings,

My best advice for you today is on the subject of abuse. To abuse is to hurt or misuse someone. It can be done mentally, physically and/or emotionally. Either way it is wrong and not to be tolerated. First of all, if you are reading this book you are old enough to act for yourself if some sick adult is abusing you. If you are being abused mentally and/or emotionally, it may be harder to tell so just know that if words or actions hurt, confuse or anger you, there is something wrong. You need to go to a responsible adult and tell. Do not keep feelings bottled up inside. The pressure may lead you to commit some act that might negatively affect the rest of your life. Responsible adults you can turn to include teachers, counselors, your religious leader and the police. Don't be afraid or ashamed because you have done nothing wrong. Just don't let a day go by being mistreated by anyone.

Even though you are not an adult yet, you have rights and you don't deserve to be misused, ever, by anyone. The law is there to protect you from harmful adults. Use it.

On the other hand, do not protect abusers. If you know someone is being abused, **tell.** If you are aware of a person being abused and you do not try to help them, you're helping the abuser. Be the responsible person. **Tell.** Taking this thought further, be certain *you* don't inadvertently become an abuser. If you bully or otherwise take advantage of someone weaker than you are you are being abusive and, not to mention, cowardly. You do not want to be either of these things so don't encourage or protect an abuser and be certain you never take undue advantage of anyone, ever. This is advice that you can and should use for the rest of your life. Abusers and other destructive people come in many different shapes, sizes and situations. **Care enough about yourself to take care of yourself now and for the rest of your life.**

Have a great day!

Day 8 Journal

_____

_____

_____

_____

_____

_____

_____

_____

_____

EMPOWERMENT DAY 9

By John Baker
Edited by Margaret Ford-Taylor

Healthy Relationships

Greetings,

Today I will share my best advice regarding building and maintaining healthy relationships. This subject is so important because your entire life will evolve around relationships with others. First will be your family, parents, siblings and other relatives. Each involving a different kind of relationship. After that will come relationships with friends, school mates, teachers and administrators. The older you get, the more relationships you will add to the list such as people you work for and with. One day it may even come to involve people who work for you. At some point relationships may include a wife and children. The point is unless you plan to become a hermit and live alone, you will be involved in many, many relationships from casual to intimate and from simple to complicated during your life time. Each of these relationships will be different because people are all different, so it will be up to you to determine what you need to do to keep each relationship as sound and healthy as possible.

The one word that will apply to any and all relationships is respect. Establish, require and give respect at the beginning and throughout each and every relationship. Of course, establishing and maintaining healthy relationships first require that you feel good about who and what you are. If you have some problems in this area, get to work on them *today*. You need to feel and know that you are a valued and valuable human being deserving of the best life has to offer, including respect. Healthy self-esteem can only help you improve the relationships you are already involved in and will make you more comfortable and self-assured while establishing future healthy relationships. On the other hand, unhealthy relationships with family, friends and others can make you feel sad, angry scared, worried and many other negative emotions. Do not ignore them. Back up. Back them up. You don't have to have a close relationship with someone who makes you feel bad. You may have to be around them—at home or at school or at work—but all that's required of you is that you be respectful. You do *not* have to allow negative people and feelings into your private space.

It is your *right* to feel as good about yourself and life as you can. Healthy relationships are based on needs and wants. You establish a relationship because the other person has something you think you need or want.

That's fair because the other person will be establishing a relationship with you for the same reason. Mutual respect is the first benchmark because it will be your guiding light for *every* relationship. In close relationships, mutual trust is the next benchmark. Relationships also require work. The more you value the relationship the more you should work to show that. Don't take other people for granted. A strong and healthy relationship is a give and take relationship and don't spend time trying to make certain you are taking more than you are giving. Have a generous spirit. This is where respect and mutual trust will guide you. You think as much of yourself as the next person thinks of him/her self so you will know when you are being taken advantage of and can act accordingly but don't look for demons. Healthy relationships have a foundation in good communication, so communicate. *Don't assume the other person knows what you are feeling.* Don't sulk and/or pout. **Communicate**. Another important skill in maintaining healthy relationships is listening. **Listen** and *hear* what the other person is trying to tell you. Finally, be a caring person. Make that a part of who you are and remember, **in order to have a good friend, you have to be one.** Good luck and God bless you.

Have a great day!

Day 9 Journal

EMPOWERMENT DAY 10

By Griffin Moore
Edited by Margaret Ford-Taylor

Conflict Resolution

Greetings,

Everyone has conflicts, meaning someone's actions, thinking or impulses differ from another person's. Depending upon the individuals involved, conflicts may be resolved very simply or they may escalate into hurt feelings, damaged relationships or worse. The point is, simple or complex, conflicts are a part of living. For everyone. What we want to deal with today are the healthiest methods of dealing with conflicting situations.

I introduce the word "healthy" because, since conflict is a part of everyday living, adopting a healthy approach can only strengthen and empower you. So, how do you feel when someone disagrees with you? Are you able to recognize that the other person is entitled to their opinion even if it differs from yours? What if you strongly disagree with the other person or they strongly disagree with you?

If the difference arouses deeply felt and negative feelings such as anger or encourages viciousness or the desire to hurt or punish, it's time for conflict resolution skills. Actually, consider making these skills a firm part of character. How? You, alone, will first know how you feel about a difference of opinion. You, alone, will first know that the difference is affecting you emotionally. It is at this initial moment when you are totally in charge of you that you move to take charge of the situation. The first step is to RECOGNIZE. Know yourself well enough, and be alert enough of your surroundings, to recognize when emotions, yours or the other persons, are about to take charge of the situation. Take physical action out of the equation. Watch for non-verbal communication from the other person. When people are letting their emotions take over, there are usually many unintentional physical clues and signs. Watch for them. Immediately, DE-STRESS. Go to your emotional safe/calm zone.

It is your individual decision in terms of what works for you. Find out *before* you need it. Is there a thought, a song, a place that immediately calms you? Some people use humor but whatever non-violent position works for you, personally, go there.

LISTEN. You may still disagree with the person but it will put you in a good place to have let them get their feelings/thoughts out.

When you do speak make certain it is specifically about the subject. **Do not insult**. **Do not hurt**. **Do not get personal**. Those are all losing positions. **Do not go to "any lengths" to win the argument**. Is it truly worth it? Can you say, *"I don't agree with you but you have the right to feel as you do.?"* If you can, no matter what position you have taken, you have won.

Have a great day!

Day 10 Journal

_____

_____

_____

_____

_____

_____

_____

_____

_____

Empowerment Day 11

By Jim Ramm
Edited by Margaret Ford-Taylor

Entrepreneurship

Greetings,

My best advice for you today concerns entrepreneurship which is the wave of the future. Social Entrepreneurship can be defined as *"establishing an enterprise or business with the aim of making a difference in society and / or the lives of those who come into contact with that business."* This is what I've devoted my life to the last several years and I've become quite successful at it. I've started a business helping people restore their health naturally without dangerous drugs or surgery and I've helped many people reverse chronic health conditions that the average M.D. will tell you are incurable. The great thing is that I'm able to do it simply with nutrition! Many people have a much better quality of life after working with me. What's even better is that my business is built around the 'network marketing' model which means that I've helped others establish their own business just like mine so that they are able to help their friends, family and acquaintances as well. This form of business is one of the purest types of businesses ever devised and is taught in the Harvard School of Business. I prefer Network Marketing or MLM (Multi-level Marketing) to any other form or entrepreneurialism because of the many advantages it has over other types of businesses. Here are a few:

• Low startup cost (less than $1,000 in most cases)
• The ability to have experienced coaches to assist you at no cost:
• **You can build it part-time while working a 'regular' job**
• **It can be built any where**
• **You're in business for yourself but not by yourself**
• **You can generate a residual income that pays you indefinitely**
  • **Your business can be passed on to your children or anyone you choose**

There are many more advantages to Network Marketing but far too many to mention in the small space I've been allotted. However, one of the most important benefits is that Network Marketing can literally allow you to write your own paycheck! In just six months my business was paying me twice as much as my police pension was! In the best opportunities you'll have a proven system and veterans in the business who have a vested interest in your becoming successful. Network Marketing is great for the distributors as well as the companies who provide the products as the normal costs of advertising and customer education are provided by the distributor force through word of mouth that saves millions of dollars that can then be directed to the distributor force in the form of commissions. Another interesting fact is that Network Marketing produces more millionaires than any other form of business. People can start a new business at any time but, honestly, the sooner the better. Statistics show that most college graduates never find work in their chosen fields, but by the time they graduate they're saddled with a mountain of student loans that will take years to pay off. It's my belief that most college age people would be better served by seriously building a business for the four to five years normally spent in college and by the end of that time they will have created an income that could pay cash for their college education if they still wished to go to college. That income stream would most likely dwarf what they would earn if they were able to find a job in their chosen profession. I recommend the videos *"Brilliant Compensation"* by Tim Sales, *"The Four-Year Career"* by Richard Bliss Brooke and *"Rise of the Entrepreneur"* by Eric Worre to get a real handle on why Network Marketing is far superior to the '40x40x40 plan.'

In case you're not familiar with that term it means to work forty hours per week for forty years and then retire on forty per cent of what you couldn't live on in the first place. Trust me, I've done that and it doesn't work! The trouble is that by the time most people find out, it is difficult to change things and get a 'redo'! A far better idea is to determine what you want to accomplish in life, what changes you want to make in society and what kind of lifestyle you want to live and then find a 'vehicle' that can get you to that destination. Figure out what you want to do and determine that nothing, or no one will keep you from accomplishing it. I recommend the following books to help you; *"Don't Let Anyone Steal Your Dream"* by Dexter Yager, *"The Four-Year Career"* by Richard Bliss Brooke (yes, it's a book and a video), *"The Motivation Manifesto"* by Brendon Burchard. Also, anything by Og Mandino, Dr. Norman Vincent Peale and Napoleon Hill will get you pointed in the right direction. You need to ask yourself this question, ***"Do I want to spend my life working to make someone else's dream come true, or do I want to spend my life doing something I love that also helps others as well as society in general?"*** *As a network marketing entrepreneur, you'll get what you want by helping others get what they want* – it's the best 'Win-Win' you could hope for. You're limited only by your imagination. I'd love to speak with you about it! ***YOU CAN DO IT!***

Sgt. Jim Ramm (retired)
1.614.874.6663
jim@yourdiyhealth.com
www.yourdiyhealth.com
www.truthfrequencyradio.com

Have a great day!

Day 11 Journal

_____

_____

_____

_____

_____

_____

_____

_____

_____

_____

EMPOWERMENT DAY 12

By Terrance Phillips Jr.
Edited by Margaret Ford-Taylor

Self-Respect

Greetings,

My best advice for you today concerns self-respect. This is one of the hardest topics because it provides the foundation for success in all of the other topics. A very wise man once said, "Until you value yourself, you won't value your time and until you value your time, you will not do anything with it." Value yourself is the key. Do you? Take a good honest look at yourself and answer the question for yourself. Do *you* value yourself? One of the overriding themes in many of the letters in this book is how important it is that you know how one-of-a-kind special you are. That doesn't mean being conceited and selfish and running over other people to have your own way. It means you have been put here on this earth to accomplish something special that only you can do. It means as a teenager it is time for you to begin to prepare yourself for adulthood in a positive, meaningful way and the only way you can accomplish this is from a positive position of a healthy sense of self.

If anything has happened to date to make you not feel good about yourself, *now* is the time to fix it. You have to feel good about yourself. That doesn't mean you won't have doubts and questions and it doesn't mean you won't make mistakes. But with high self-esteem you will know that whatever problems arise you can find the answers. You will know that to have value yourself you don't have to follow others or put others down. With high self-esteem you will feel free to lead a clean, sober life and strive for all that is good and positive. As Eleanor Roosevelt once said you will know that, "you not only have the right to be an individual, you have an obligation to be one."

Of course, you are not an adult yet but you're not a little kid either. There will be help along the way if you look for it, positive help from caring and responsible adults. Try not to waste your time hero worshiping. It's time for you to prepare yourself to become a hero. The first step is self-assessment. Go in your room or to a quiet space such as in a library. Make list "A" which will be all of the positive things you like about yourself no matter how small they may seem. Be honest. Everything is important because it's a part of who you are. If possible, read over that list at least once a day. Now make another list headed "B" and write down all of things you would like to change or improve about yourself.

Study that list and make certain that what you want to improve or change will make you a better you, not someone else. Develop a "how to" plan for list "B" that will allow you to begin to work on self-improvement. Work on that every day until the things on List "B" can be transferred to list "A". Now please know, if you start to change or start acting differently than you have in the past, people will react in different ways. You can't please everybody, and everyone won't appreciate you. Be prepared for that but don't let it stop you. It's okay. If someone doesn't like you, make it their loss. Your concern is making you the best and healthiest *you* you can, physically, mentally and emotionally. Someone who feels really good about who they are. It's important that you concentrate on the good things about you. Accept who you are. Without sacrificing others, always decide what is right and best for you and then follow through. Don't let others opinion of you be your guide. Always try to focus on the positive. If you focus on the positive, you will get more positive results. One thing I can guarantee, if you focus on the negative you will *always* receive the negative. So, avoid a "poor me" victim mentality. It only accents how little you value yourself. Use the good things about yourself to succeed. You'll find the more success you have just being you the better you will feel about yourself. No matter how hard you try, things will go wrong sometimes. That's natural but when you fail, fall or make a mistake take responsibility for your actions, learn what ever lesson you can from the experience, pick yourself up and forge ahead. Always resist anger. It's a negative and the only person it will hurt is you. Always look for the humor in a situation. It's a positive that can defuse many emotional situations. There isn't a person living who hasn't made mistakes. The point is to learn from them and use the experience as a character building block. You can have an exciting, productive future ahead. It's really up to you. I don't say it will be easy. But you can do it. The greater the challenge, the greater the feeling of success will be. So, get started! The world is waiting! Just for you!

Have a great day!

Day 12 Journal

_____

_____

_____

_____

_____

_____

_____

_____

_____

_____

EMPOWERMENT DAY 13

By Brian Barnes
Edited by Margaret Ford-Taylor

Education

Greetings,

A formal definition of education is, "Knowledge, skills or cultivation acquired through instruction or study." In times gone by there were many successful "self-educated" men, most of whom did not even have the benefit of a high school diploma. There were those who through years of self-planned instruction and study, hard times and luck finally led lives of achievement and prosperity. For all intents and purposes, those times are gone. Today, to enter most fields, a high school diploma *plus* education beyond high school or, a higher education, is a must. In fact, almost without exception, you will find that whatever you desire to learn about, become proficient and expert in, a course of study has been designed to guide you once you complete high school. So hopefully, after completing high school, your plan is to a pursue higher education. Now, when we think of "higher" education, we usually think of going to college when in actual fact, there are other perfectly legitimate avenues to a higher education such as trade schools and apprenticeships.

There are long lists of careers in the medical field, cosmetology and business, among others, that require Certificates of Completion instead of degrees. Any number of factors might prevent one from attending college. Some of us may even decide that a formal college setting does not suit us. However, everyone *should* decide how they plan to earn a living what they are most interested in doing with the rest of their lives. They should then chart a course to learn as much about the subject as they can and how they can become an expert in their chosen field. This is also "higher" education. How you go about achieving this becomes a personal decision. The point is, in order to successfully compete in today's highly complex and technological society, you should plan to extend your education beyond high school.

In considering *all* of the options, a formal college plan should, of course, be. Pursuing this track and depending upon what field you want to consider as well as what your end goal is determined to be there are two and four-year college degrees followed by the Masters and Doctorate degrees. Due to their complexity, some fields may require even further study. Again, these are decisions that only you can finally make.

You'll find the majority of young people who plan to attend college, consider a four-year degree in a chosen field sufficient for entering the work force because this is the minimum requirement for many of today's jobs. Needless to say, the higher the degree the greater the chance for employment in most markets and salaries are usually commiserate with degrees since the degree is used as an indicator of the level of proficiency in the chosen field. Learning all that you can will help you become a more valuable employee and a better person.

You know within yourself what is positive, solid, sensible and lawful BUT if there is even a shadow of a doubt, say NO! The second response to any doubtful decisions is, "I'll think about it." If you are pressured in any way to make a quick decision or a decision of the moment, don't do it. Other than life and death decisions where human survival instincts will kick in, any decision worth making, is worth taking the time to give serious thought.

Have a great day!

Day 13 Journal

_____

_____

_____

_____

_____

_____

_____

_____

_____

_____

Empowerment Day 14

By Dameon Walker
Edited by Margaret Ford-Taylor

Self-Esteem

Greetings,

Today I want to discuss self-esteem,

In order to build and maintain a positive sense of who you are, it is important to understand the contributing factors that influence self-esteem. Some of these are the images in the media or advertising, the opinions of our friends and family and the willingness or ability to learn and grow from life experiences. The most important thing to know about advertising is its purpose which is to convince the consumer (viewer, listener, reader, etc.) that "they" know what's best for you and in order to be happy, successful and wealthy one needs to be like the images "they" are presenting. Often, these messages serve to make young men feel as if they are inadequate and not valued for who they are but only for what they possess. This is not true. You are important, valuable and unique based on who you are as a person not on what you possess or how closely you resemble someone on TV.

Instead of trying to "fit in" and be like someone else, you will be much happier in life if you spend that energy being comfortable with who you really are and focusing on the things that make you happy and comfortable. If you always compare yourself and base your value relative to someone else's possessions, and or looks you will always have low self-esteem. it is important to love yourself for who you are, to value your uniqueness and only internalize those messages that contribute to building a positive self-esteem.

The more you love yourself, the more difficult it is for anyone to make you feel you're not valuable. That is **the secret** to having a healthy and positive self-esteem. Friends and family also play an important role in building a young man's self-esteem. Ideally, those who are closest to us should be our primary sources of love, positivity and support. As children we look to adults to teach us the difference between right and wrong, to demonstrate how we are supposed to behave, to display unconditional love and to support us in our development as we grow and attempt to become productive members of our communities. However, as we grow to be young men we begin to see and hear things from adults that contradict the love, support and positivity they are supposed to provide. At this point it is very important to develop the ability to continue to internalize the positive and supportive elements from interactions with others while **dismissing** those behaviors that do not contribute to uplifting and loving perceptions of yourself. It's called **growing up**. As a teenager, this is probably where you are now. This is also where the real work begins because it can be very difficult to prevent the negative opinions and behaviors of those you love from having an impact on your self-image. Even so, **try to remember that what someone else thinks about you is far less important than what you think about yourself**. This does not mean that you should never listen to others. It means you should be open to *constructive* opinions from people who have your interests at heart and ignore *destructive* criticism, so it does not impact your positive perceptions of yourself. <u>You should make every effort to spend more time with those who contribute to your life in a positive manner.</u> This may be difficult because some of the people you love the most may be some of the most *emotionally destructive* people in your life.

However, you can always love them but do not spend a lot of time with them because they WILL hurt you and prevent you from building a loving, positive self-image. Finally, you must develop the ability to learn from your experiences as well as from the experiences of others. Far too often young men make the same mistakes which suggest they are unwilling to, or incapable of self-reflection. You will have negative experiences at some point(s) in your life.

Everyone experiences setbacks, let downs, failures and losses. The only difference between those who are emotionally weakened long term by these experiences is the ability to reflect on the circumstances and LEARN from them. By learn I mean **DO NOT** repeat the same mistakes. Aside from the negative impact to your self-esteem, making the same mistakes diminishes the trust/confidence you have in yourself to be successful. Also, learning is not restricted to your own experiences but also include learning from the experiences of others. One way to do this is to *read* what has been written about others and then apply the knowledge to your own life in a positive way. **The point is to never stop learning. Observe, listen and learn.** The more knowledge you have, the less susceptible you will be to destructive thoughts and behaviors and the more receptive you will be to those positive inputs in your life that will contribute to a healthy, loving and positive self-image.

Have a great day!

Day 14 Journal

_____

_____

_____

_____

_____

_____

_____

_____

_____

EMPOWERMENT DAY 15

By Anonymous
Edited by Margaret Ford-Taylor

Peer-Pressure

Greetings,

Teenagers can be overwhelmingly responsible when they are given time and the resources to respond to a particular idea or situation. In immediate and social situations, however, too often it's another story. With this age group the influence of others, especially peers, is strong. It's known as peer-pressure. It's when others think and express how they feel you should look, dress, think and respond to life and its challenges. Of course, it is not exclusive to this age group but it is certainly strongest. This group has just completed the phase of their life where parents and other guardians have made all of the final decisions. For the first time they may find themselves in position after position requiring them to make decisions on their own about what they will and will not do. This is when lessons learned in the first twelve years of life should provide a foundation for the kinds of decisions one has to make.

However, with or without that foundation, sooner or later every teen finds him or herself in this position where they will have to begin making decisions that they and they alone are responsible for. My advice for you today is this: The first thing to recognize when responding to peer-pressure is that your friends are at the same crossroads in life that you are. They don't know either. They are responding to life just as you are. So, if the advice is positive, solid, sensible and lawful, by all means take it. This might fall under the category known as "positive peer-pressure." Peer-pressure that can be neither positive nor negative may be as mild as wearing certain clothes because most of the people you associate with on a regular basis dress a certain way. There is absolutely nothing wrong with bowing to this sort of peer pressure as long as the clothes you select are clothes that *you* like, clothes that fit *your* personality and *your* physique, clothes that you feel totally comfortable in. Be aware that you are still learning important attributes such as self-control, looking ahead and thinking for yourself. You will gradually leave the peer-pressure behind that comes with these life lessons along with your teen years. Too often, however, it is negative peer-pressure that moves teens into making decisions that may follow them to and through their adult years. The most offensive of these include bullying others, sex and drug and alcohol abuse and other risky behavior.

You know within yourself what is positive, solid, sensible and lawful BUT if there is even a shadow of a doubt, say NO! In the case of behavior such as bullying, there is an age old biblical reference that carries the right answer every time. Simply treat others the way that you wish to be treated. Period. ANYTHING that goes against that decision is wrong. After NO, the second response to any doubtful decisions is, "I'LL THINK ABOUT IT." If you are pressured in any way to make a quick decision or a decision of the moment, don't do it. If you are with a group and a decision makes you the slightest bit uncomfortable, find a safe way to LEAVE. Other than life and death decisions where human survival instincts will kick in, any decision worth making, is worth taking the time to give serious thought. It's worth researching. It's worth consulting a responsible adult, a teacher, a youth worker, a church leader, your parent who cares about what happens to you than anyone. You may be ridiculed or otherwise pressured by teen peers but stick to your guns. People who attempt to pressure you into doing what they think is best for you, have a problem themselves. Don't let their problem become your problem. Do not let others decide what is best for you. I promise you, as an adult you will congratulate yourself on your past maturity and wisdom and I guarantee you, you will have missed nothing worthwhile. Instead, you might find you have saved yourself endless heartache. Contrary to what your "acquaintance" has told you, trying a drug that someone has convinced you is harmless or "fun" CAN make you an addict for life. It CAN end your life on that first try. Okay, maybe the second one. Or maybe the third one. Or--never mind. You are now addicted. Now you will lie, steal, cheat, sacrifice yourself and all you hold dear for something you never planned to do or be in the first place. Look around you. There are examples of what you do NOT want to become all around you. Why do it in the first place? Oh! Peer-pressure. Have sense enough to be afraid of certain things. Throughout your life things will frighten you. Only a fool is afraid of nothing. It is not fear that's a no-no. It's what fear leads you to DO that determines whether you are a coward, a hero or simply a fool. Be a hero. If you *DO* fall, pick yourself up and try again. It will be harder this time but you can do it. If things go sour again, start again. And again and again and again.

In the meantime, here are some tips negotiating negative peer-pressure. Decide and know who and what you are. Set values and goals for yourself. Decide what lines you will not cross for anyone. Decide what past times you will save until you are an adult. Actually, knowing that you are still a child is the first step toward adulthood. How you feel, what you think, decide and choose is very important and remember it's

YOUR decision because as long as the universe has been in existence, no one has ever looked, felt or thought like you. No one ever will. That makes you unique. Unique objects are valued beyond measure. You are unique and valuable beyond measure. Know that. Work and live to perfect that ideology. Use it as your guide and measuring device. Take the high road. Modestly but determinedly. Decide not to let anything or anyone deter you from the high pursuits you set for yourself. Be true to self. Value the things and the people you love and who love you. Be yourself. Remember, you are unique. Be the best *you* you can be. Be honest about it. It's okay. You are growing up. You are allowed. From this vantage point you can listen to all the advice someone cares to give. You can select what is good for *you* and reject the rest. Believe me, you have all the time in the world, which is the rest of your life, to make tough decisions. My advice to you is, take it. All the time in the world.

Have a great Day!

Day 15 Journal

_____

_____

_____

_____

_____

_____

_____

_____

_____

EMPOWERMENT DAY 16

By Perry Sanders
Edited by Margaret Ford-Taylor

Money

Greetings,

Everyone uses, wants and thinks about money because in today's society, it's the way we get the things we need and want. Also, I have found that among teenagers there is some confusion about the best way to get this necessary commodity called money. Today, we set the record straight. You need money to survive, to live, to prosper and the ONLY sane approach to getting it is by earning it through education, hard work and proper management, NOT 1) thinking you're going to become a rap artist; 2) NOT thinking you're going to be a sports star; 3) NOT thinking you're going into become a movie star; 4) NOT thinking you're going to hit the lottery; 5) NOT selling drugs; 6) NOT waiting for your parents to die and leave you their money. If you are reading this letter then you are old enough to start using the advice in it. One of the most important money tips you should begin to invest in right now is education. This includes the formal education you are receiving now as well as the informal education which comes from learning by doing. Begin to look at each task you undertake as a part of your on-going education. Listen: Once you learn something, no one can take it away from you. Think about it. That's Math, Science, English, a foreign language, a musical instrument, how to fix a car, how to stop a leaky faucet, how to cut hair and on and on and on and on. Learn, learn, learn. At school and away from school. I repeat, once you learn something, no one can take it away from you. You can build on it and make it more, bigger, better but this is something you now have as a foundation for many things including making money. You get money for providing a job or service. You don't *make* money. You *earn* money because you can do something that somebody wants. My next point is about hard work. Don't be afraid to do more. If you are asked to go a mile, go two. If you are asked to jump, jump high. If asked to jump high, jump higher. Whatever you are asked to do or whatever you undertake, show that you have the maturity and the wisdom to know the value of hard work. Everyone wants an employee or partner who's willing to carry his share of the load or more if he has to. The final point is management. Again, you are old enough to begin managing your money however small the amount. People become rich because they know how to manage their money. If you have a job or some other steady income, ask a parent or some other responsible adult to help you open an account. Pledge an amount to deposit each week. Be honest and strict with yourself. If after a time you decide you have pledged too much, cut it down but whatever amount you *do* decide to save, save it. Don't cheat. If you want to save for something specific, use another saving source for that. The main savings should have a time such as high school graduation or some other milestone in your life and this is just a "check-in" time. *Always* maintain a savings account. Even if you don't have a regular job. An untouchable savings account. No matter how small, it will give you so much more than the amount. It will teach you discipline. It will give you pride knowing the many choices you could make with the money but instead you have the strength of purpose to know what is better for you to do.

Anybody can buy. There is *always* something to be bought but can you save when you don't absolutely have to buy? There will also be a greater value for what you eventually spend your money on. Having money does not compare with having love and good health but it is important so plan and live your life accordingly.

Have a great day!

Day 16 Journal

_____

_____

_____

_____

_____

_____

_____

_____

_____

_____

EMPOWERMENT DAY 17

By Gary Lee Collins
Edited by Margaret Ford-Taylor

Dating

Greetings,

An official definition for the word "dating" is *a planned social occasion with a member of the opposite sex.*" It is my opinion that any official "dating" under the age of 16 should be in groups with adult supervision. As a teen under the age of 16 you should have about a million considerations before you get to dating. At 16 and over you should have about two million considerations before you get to dating but we'll discuss those later. Of course you will and should be interested in the opposite sex long before you turn 16. It's normal. It's natural. BUT If you *are* interested in one on one dating, then you are also mature enough to know there is nothing to be done about it until you're older. You *can* have a relationship, which should begin with a friendship, whenever you and a girl decide to do so. A friendship can have many, many outlets including one on one face to face conversations; conversations via phone, electronic media, etc, visits to each other's homes; birthday and holiday celebrations; correspondence through letters, cards, etc. A friendship can last for years until you're both ready to start dating formally and a friendship has many advantages, the strongest of which is it gives couples a chance to really get to know each other. You are growing up. She is growing up. A "friendship" period gives you both a chance to go beyond physical attributes and find out if interests and values remain in common. Earlier in this correspondence, I indicated you will have much more on your mind after age 16 than you did before. Let's be clear about that. You *should* have a focus on school, not dating. You *should* have a focus on "after" school. Is that higher education? Embarking on a trade? Getting a job? Are you planning to stay with your parents? Get an apartment? Take a trip to the moon? What exactly are you planning to do with the next 50 years of your life? If no one else thinks about that, you should. It's your life. Back to the subject of official dating. Self-discipline is a key word here. Yes, your hormones are acting up like crazy. I hope it help to let you know that since the beginning of time every man who has ever lived had hormone's that began acting up like crazy at just about your age. It makes you a little nuts sometimes, right? It gets you excited at times. At other times it scares you. Other times it makes you want to pound your chest and act like Tarzan.

The female body becomes the most mysterious, the most intriguing, the most captivating phenomenon ever known to mankind. Sometimes it feels as if you're experiencing something new and different from everybody else. Too often, you're miserable and confused. It's the hormones. Scientifically, physically, mentally, emotionally it means your body is preparing itself to produce children. It's hormonal. Your feelings are real but other than that, they have nothing to do with actual reality. Stop a minute and think. Every animal species has a way of perpetuating itself. What makes human beings different from all other animals is we are endowed with the powers of thought and reason among other attributes. NOW is one of those times when it is important to use those powers of thought and reason. If you are going to date, THINK about it and at least know WHY you are dating. Do not confuse strong biological urges (which is all about YOU) with love (which is mostly about the other person.)

Of course, socialization is a very important part of growing up. Knowing how to interact with the opposite sex is also an important part of growing up but there are alternatives to formal dating such as: Friendships, male and female, school work, school activities, hobbies, sports and cold showers; social activities of a religious and/or civic connection, serious planning about your future and sports and cold showers. I repeat, your feelings are real but they have nothing to do with reality.

Be smart. Use your teen years to seek answers not add complications. Plan to leave the physical stuff until you are mature enough to handle ALL aspects of dating, including the financial. Now, if you are this teenager who has the money and the time, your head's screwed on straight, you know exactly what you are doing and why and your futures all laid out clearly in front of you and you decide to date formally, here are some tips. Actually, they are tips you can use in any case. First of all, make certain of your personal hygiene. Bathe and brush your teeth. Many a romance has died before it can be born because someone got in a hurry. Secondly, there is no adage better or older than the one that says, treat her (or anyone) the way you want to be treated, with honesty and respect. The basic manners you learned as a first grader still works now. Dating is too varied and complex for a specific "How To" manual. Let it suffice here to say, If you've gotten to the point of asking for a formal date, there was something that attracted you to her in the first place. If she accepted, there was something about you that she found attractive or at least interesting. Build on that. Plan the date as well as you can with her in mind BUT be yourself. In case you've heard differently, being the strongest of the couple will never go out of style. Take care of her.

Treat her the way you would insist that someone treat your sister. Finally, since you are both teenagers an absolute law is, **YOU MUST HAVE FUN!**

Have a great day!

Day 17 Journal

Empowerment Day 18

By Jesus Flores
Edited by Margaret Ford-Taylor

Abuse

Greetings,

You've heard it before but since it's the best advice about the subject that's ever been given, I'll say it again. **"JUST SAY, NO!"** I will add, **THE FIRST TIME, THE NEXT TIME AND EVERY TIME!** Of course it's a million times harder to stop using drugs than it is to not start in the first place. Also, most teens with substance abuse problems began using drugs or alcohol as a result of peer-pressure. So make it a policy, today, to **"JUST SAY, NO! Every time**. I guarantee you that those same people who may have pressured you to start will not be there once you have a problem. They're not necessarily bad people. So, don't look at outward appearance as an indication. They may be teenagers finding their way-growing up–like you. Become the leader in this regard. **Say, NO!** If the pressure is too great, you'll find plenty of other teens who feel the way you do. Seek them out. Hang with them. On the other hand, the adult who encourages you to drink or take drugs *is* a bad person.

That person does not have your best interest at heart. Avoid them at all costs.

Next, know this, the brain is a powerful instrument. You are absolutely and totally in charge of *everything* you say or do *before* you drink or take drugs. After you drink or take drugs your brain readjusts itself to take in this new phenomenon. It is a pleasurable sensation. As you progress, it progresses. First, without your help, the brain says you WANT the drug, that pleasurable sensation again. Next, you'll NEED the drug. Finally, you'll HAVE TO HAVE the drug. You won't feel complete without it. As a matter of fact, nothing else will matter more than the drug. Not your health. Not your family. Not your education. Not your finances. Not your future. Nothing. There are those who will say, "It can't hurt to try one time." Someone may even tell you how many times they have 'gotten high' and gotten away with it. The ones who won't tell you those stories, can't. **They're dead or at least brain dead.** I wonder what they would say to you if their wonderful brain was still functioning. They would say, it's a fool's choice. You have to admit that among other consequences it's just plain stupid to play Russian roulette with your life. True, when you are a teenager, it feels as it life will go on forever, that things like death only happens to old people or at least to other people. Check the internet.

Get the statistics. It's happening to teenagers like you every day, every hour. Good kids. Kids with a future. Be afraid! Be afraid for your life! Be afraid for your future! Be afraid of not being here, not existing! This is a good fear. It's a fear that says you are beginning to grow up. You are beginning to think like a man. You are beginning to think for and about yourself. You begin to think about how your behavior affects those around you, those you care about and who care about you. The child assumes some adult will take care of everything. On the threshold, you're beginning to realize that that adult is you. Perhaps you have already started drinking and taking drugs. You can stop. This is not to say it will be easy but you *can* stop. Addiction is a disease, a relapsing disease. A person may have to try over and over again but you *can* stop if you want to badly enough. It's up to you. You had no say-so about coming into this world nor about what has happened to you in your early life. Now you do have say-so. **You have choices**. It's *your* mind and *your* body. Now that you are becoming an adult it's increasingly more *your* responsibility to take care of them. That's what this letter is also about. Becoming an adult. You can decide not to do drugs. You can decide to stop if you've started. Either way, you'll find help along the way if you reach out for it.

The important point here is it is time for you to begin taking control of that wonderful gift that's been given to you, the gift of life.   You've got everything it takes, You know within yourself what is positive, solid, sensible and lawful BUT if there is even a shadow of a doubt, **say NO!**   The second response to any doubtful decisions is, "I'll think about it."   If you are pressured in any way to make a quick decision or a decision of the moment, don't do it. Other than life and death decisions where human survival instincts will kick in, any decision worth making is worth taking the time to give serious thought.   **So go for it!**

Have a great day!

Day 18 Journal

EMPOWERMENT DAY 19

By Diaz R. Walker
Edited by Margaret Ford-Taylor

Healthy Hygiene

Greetings,

This book is to, for and about teenage boys like you so it's important that a subject which greatly affects teenage boys like you should be addressed. It is a noticeable part of the cycle of life called puberty. Actually, the dictionary definition of puberty is, *"the period during which an individual becomes physiologically capable of reproduction."* It means, with the cooperation of a female, you are now capable of producing a child. Subsequently, your hormones go into overdrive and all kinds of seemingly weird things begin to happen to your mind and body which are many, many more conversations unto themselves and will not be addressed today. In this particular letter to you, I give strong advice about healthy hygiene because with puberty hygiene takes on a life of its own and past hygiene regimens are no longer enough.

Before you became a teenager, the adults in your life made certain you had baths so that you could be clean and neat along with being healthy and happy. It is a totally different ballgame now and it's all *your* responsibility.

Among other things, with puberty, you begin to sweat a lot, your body produces more oil and hair now grows in unusual places such as under your arms, on your legs, and around your genitals which, in that location, bears the name, pubic hair. Establish and put into practice a good personal and consistent hygiene routine. The operative word here is consistent. Know that bathing and or showering *at least* once a day with hot water and soap is not an option. You must bathe. Often. Deodorant without the aid of soap and water will not work. You will only set yourself up to get embarrassed. Publically. Do invest in a good deodorant that you use *only* after washing thoroughly. When washing, pay close and extra attention to those areas of your body where glands produce sweat at a prolific and alarming rate. That's the underarm and public hair areas where the body produces more bacteria more frequently than other areas If you do not wash these areas daily and thoroughly you will smell bad. **Not cute. Not funny. Not mature. Just bad. You must bathe. Again, often.**

In your teenage years, your feet become more active. Sports and every day walking demand frequent changing of socks. In fact, try to change into fresh clothes, especially underwear and socks, every day. Take responsibility for making certain your clothes are kept clean and orderly. Pack an extra Tee shirt in your book bag.

When you get home after gym or other physical activity, take all sports clothes out of your gym bag so it can air out. To aid in keeping the bag fresh, spray it weekly. Another tip. Help mom. Change and wash your own bed linen weekly. It will be good practice for when you have your own apartment later on. Make a personal commitment to consistent and healthy hygiene. Before you consider dating. It's one of the first signs of moving from boyhood to manhood. You'll be glad that you did and so will everyone you come into contact with.

Have a great day!

Day 19 Journal

EMPOWERMENT DAY 20

By Anonymous
Edited by Margaret Ford-Taylor

Suicide

Greetings,

Today I will share my best advice on the topic of suicide. I know that it works because it has saved my life for many years now. The first thing I will say to you is STOP! For just a few minutes, **STOP** considering suicide as an option and concentrate on this letter. It is important that you put aside the idea of suicide, at least temporarily, because once you allow yourself to commit the act, it is FOREVER. The outcome of suicide is death. You won't exist. No changing your mind. After suicide, no problem can be solved because death, again, is forever. I do not believe you actually want to not exist any longer. You want whatever the problem is to be solved. You want to be happy and enjoy your life. Am I right? Well, know that you *can* and *should* enjoy life BUT you have to LIVE in order to do that. So, let's talk about how you can solve your problems and live. The motto that I, and many others, live by and has saved many, many lives is **"LIVE ONE DAY AT A TIME."**

Life can seem to be, and can actually be, overwhelming at times. Sometimes it is necessary to take it in small bite-sized pieces. This is especially true because, as a teenager, many problems may seem non-solve able because so many adults control your life. Take a deep breath and know, you will not be a teenager forever. As a matter of fact, teen years are very, very short when you look at a life time. Most of those years, you and only you, will be in charge of you and how you handle life but for now you mostly have to depend upon the adults in your life. So, let's look at one of the most serious considerations first. Are you being physically abused in any way? If so, report it! Report it! Report it! Report it! The person is committing a crime and you are a victim. Do not be afraid or ashamed. It is not your fault. I repeat, you are a victim. Tell a responsible adult. Go to your school counselor or a teacher that you trust. Look online for a phone number or just walk into a police station. The point is, TELL!

Next, if you are not being abused, the situation is still serious if you think suicide is an option. IT IS NOT. The second motto you want to commit to memory is, THIS TOO, SHALL PASS. Take it one day at a time and know that *every* problem has a solution and as long as you are *alive* things can get better. They *will* get better. I promise. First, begin to realize *now* how important you are.

Since the beginning of time, no one has ever looked, thought, felt like you. Until the end of time, no one ever will. That makes you unique. Special. Invaluable. One of a kind. There is something *you* are supposed to do in life that *no one* can accomplish but you. Now-these teenage years is the time you have to prepare to do that every special something. So *treasure* yourself. Take care of yourself, your body, your mind. Remind yourself of this every day. You don't have time to die, to not exist. You are in your preparation period for all the great things to come. You are a miracle created by God, the creator of the universe. How cool is that? You are stronger than you know. Being able to communicate about what bothers you is important. If you don't have an outlet, a close friend, do look for that caring, responsible adult. Something that will never fail you is a journal. Get in the habit of putting your thoughts in a journal every day. Pick a time each day when you can record those things that help, depress, inspire, overwhelm or comfort you. Write, draw, express yourself. It is so important that you don't let feelings just bottle up inside until you finally become desperate. Physical exercise, running or just walking can do so much to help your one-day-at-a-time resolution. Are there things about yourself you don't like or that you want to change? Any improvement is possible. Make a list, study it and work on it. Don't give in to it.

Keep yourself physically and mentally clean, healthy and fit. Kick depression in the butt and out of the door. I challenge you to find the courage, the strength, the tenacity and the fight to push through each day's obstacles. You can do it. You can do anything, accomplish anything you want as long as you are alive. Congratulate yourself every night and begin again with the new day. Finally, if you are convinced you have given these thoughts your best effort and it's just not working, please tell your parents so they can seek medical support. Your condition may just be physical. Whatever you do, don't give up. Life is precious. And remember, I am with you, loving you, caring for you every step of the way. You are not alone.

Have a great, great day!

Day 20 Journal

_____

_____

_____

_____

_____

_____

_____

_____

_____

_____

EMPOWERMENT DAY 21

By Charles G. Copeland
Edited by Margaret Ford-Taylor

Self-Respect

Greetings,

Today I would like to share my best advice regarding self-respect. It's simply this. People who have a good opinion of themselves give off a certain tell-tell sign of appreciation and that's how they treat others also. If you treat yourself well, you will not have a problem treating others with respect. It is a proven fact that when you like you, you have no hesitation extending kindness, graciousness and respect to others. When you treat others like "crap" you automatically tell the world that you really don't like yourself. Self-respect begins from within and then extends outwards. To keep that self-respect, you must nurture it. You have to learn to be comfortable in your own skin because those attributes that make you unique are enough. Always work hard, do your part, be clean, kind, caring and generous of spirit and then don't concern yourself with how others perceive you. Just make certain *you* like you. Here's another tip. Don't compromise your values just to fit in.

Celebrate the good things about you and then grow at being the best *you you can be*. Value your time and never give up on yourself. No one can take away your self-respect but you. Earn it, cultivate it and keep it for the rest of your life.

Have a great day!

Day 21 Journal

_____

_____

_____

_____

_____

_____

_____

_____

_____

_____

EMPOWERMENT DAY 22

By Brother Umar
Edited by Margaret Ford-Taylor

Conflict Resolution

Greetings,

My best advice for you today, concerns conflict resolution. When I think of conflict resolution, I think of learning to deal with life on life's terms because you are going to have conflict because it is a normal part of life. Many days you will have bad moments. Every day is not going to be a great day in its entirety. Everybody has conflicts. It's about how you resolve the conflict that matters. The ideal is when both parties participate in a win-win situation. Failing that ideal, you must ask yourself what you need to do to resolve the conflict without aggression and without sacrificing the main goals of what you were doing *before* you entered the conflicting situation. My advice to you is to stop and think. If you are angry, find a way to get rid of that anger without getting into situations and inviting consequences that you will later regret. Think about consequences *before* you act. Find a way to get rid of the anger *before* you explode.

Finding outlets to blow off steam is a must. It can come through your senses in the form of sound, touch or taste. There are thing you can do to blow off steam like going to the gym. Whatever you decide, find your "calming spot." You get to see and hear things you wouldn't normally see or hear when you are hot headed. You'll be able to read those verbal and nonverbal cues that could possible save your life. Avoid aggression. Aggression scares people and may scare them into acting even more aggressive than you. Do what my granddad taught me to do. Stop and count to ten. It may just save your live or save you from ten plus years in prison. As simple as it sounds, count to ten before you lose your temper. If you are still angry, count to ten again. Having an adult male figure as a role model is an important part of becoming a healthy adult male, physically, mentally and emotionally. That is not always possible. It is unfortunate, but it is not always possible. Without that active person in your life, find your own positive male role models. Men who have had successful lives that included making a contribution to society. Success is NOT measured simply in money. You should certainly plan to earn enough to take care of yourself but a great measure of success includes how much you are able to contribute to those less fortunate than you.

Those role models are all around you. Look for them. You will find that, without exception, they were/are thinking men. Men who thought *before* they acted. Thinking leads to feelings and feelings lead to actions. When you leave thinking out and just go for feelings, you are setting yourself up for trouble. I will share a story that happened to me some time ago and may benefit you one day. As I was boarding the bus one day, I was letting the women and children on first when a guy behind me said, "Hey, man, are you getting on or what?" I turned around and said, "If you go home and put a dress on, I will let you on first too." Why did I say that?" I said that because he had offended me and I spoke without thinking. It did not make me feel good about myself plus now I felt I had to watch this guy because I didn't know what he would do. What I actually did was ease over to him and say, "Hey, excuse me, Sir, but as we were getting on the bus I said something I should not. Can you please forgive me?" Surprisingly enough, he was extremely gracious about it and said, "Sure. I actually did not see the kids, to be honest." We shook hands and I got off the bus. That's just a short simple story. All encounters are different. The point is, it is always wise to be aware of other people and their needs and feelings.

It's not just about you. Aggression is never the answer. Stop and think. Usually it takes more strength to be passive than assertive. Try to keep your ego in check in all situations. It will strengthen you. Pick your battles carefully. Learn from them and use each one as a lesson for conflicts to come.

Have a great day!

Day 22 Journal

Empowerment Day 23

By Quameen S. Vernon
Edited by Margaret Ford-Taylor

Self-Esteem

Greetings,

I am a firm believer that self-esteem and self-love are the foundation to living a happier life. It gives you that inner-peace you need when you feel the whole world has turned against you. When I reflect on my pre-teen and teenage years, I definitely had low self-esteem. I even struggled with it in my early twenties in certain aspects. I longed for the affirmation of someone else to make me feel better about myself. And in other times, I would wish that I could see myself as other people saw me. This came from a deeply rooted issue of never feeling good enough or smart enough and a strong fear of rejection. I also wanted to point the finger at other people and make them responsible for the way I felt. It was always because this person didn't love me enough or this person treated me this way or the girl I liked didn't see me the way I saw her. This stopped me from experiencing life.

I measured myself against people at different points in my life in such areas as what I thought I should be like, only to find out they were just as insecure as I was and had low self-esteem as well. Young man be mindful of who you are using as your yardstick. Stop comparing what you have or what you don't have to others. Compare yourself only to what you envision as being the best version of YOU! We all have the power to change or boost our self-esteem by what we think and speak of ourselves. *I had to literally tell myself that I was handsome. I had to tell myself that I was intelligent. I had to tell myself that I was special and there was no one else like me.* I started doing things that I enjoyed and not what I thought other people would think was cool. I started speaking about topics that I liked and stopped just talking about what I thought people wanted me to say. When I began to do these things is when I declared my independence It was my freedom from caring what other people thought about me because as I grew older I learned that the majority of people are followers and some eventually started following me. When I started speaking my own higher self-esteem into existence, I started believing in myself. I started believing I could accomplish certain things and took pride in doing so and wanted to see others achieve that as well because when you treat yourself good, you treat others good.

In regards to how well one is groomed and dressed, my father always told me "when you look good, you act good!" So, tell you you have higher self-esteem, you gradually start to make bold moves, you start trying new things you wouldn't have before. You must envision yourself doing it whatever it is that you want to do. Our minds our powerful tools that help shape our reality. High self-esteem produces confidence not arrogance. When I had low self-esteem, I would act out and handled my frustration in such a way that was impulsive and often destructive. When I had higher self-esteem, I controlled the situation and kept my cool I was poised. I noticed when I had lower self-esteem, I wanted other people to feel this way, so I tore them down with my words.

But when I had higher self-esteem I started to speak life into certain situations and I poured into others with my words. Make no mistake, acquiring higher self-esteem is a process because you must break down the plaque of those years of low self-esteem. But once you do, man-oh-man, the sky isn't the limit because the universe doesn't have one. Believe in yourself, young man. Love yourself young man! And my best advice to you is: Self-love is not a destination. It's a journey! Peace Kid!

Have a great day!

Day 23 Journal

Empowerment Day 24

By David N. Jacobs
Edited by Margaret Ford-Taylor

Healthy Competition

Greetings,

When competition is healthy, it can motivate, improve and inspire. When it is unhealthy it can become toxic and destructive. You want to practice healthy competition, not only for others, but also for yourself. How do you do that? Well, first, before you continue competing with others, stand in front of a full-length mirror, take a good long look and make an honest assessment of self. Yourself. In the mirror, you should find your first competitor. YOU. No one ever reaches perfection of course but as long as it is your goal, you will continue to strive for the rest of your life. That's important. So, begin a competition with your own imperfections. Set goals and begin to challenge yourself in areas of self-improvement mentally, physically and emotionally. Begin the work to develop a healthy mind. The healthy mind knows the value of a positive self-image and self-worth and works every day to be the best person one can be to achieve that end.

The healthy mind knows that when entering competition with others, the person who knows they are important and valuable can allow others to be important and valuable in their own right. The healthy mind can take whatever is being done seriously without taking itself overly serious. Moderation, even humor, are valuable life tools in all human endeavors. Even as the healthy mind won't brag when it wins nor sulk when it loses, engages all powers to win, it will still appreciate excellence, honest effort and skill in others. The healthy mind can give competitors their due. It is at this point of knowledge and self-awareness that one begins to engage in healthy competition with others. The point, in competing of course, is to win. However, it is critical that winning is taken in perspective. Winning is certainly a goal in healthy competition but just as important, in any endeavor, *is the journey*. Safeguard, value and learn from each journey. Make yourself your biggest, best and strongest competitor and in so doing you will make every competition, not only healthy, but a guaranteed winner every time.

Have a great day!

Day 24 Journal

EMPOWERMENT DAY 25

By Michael K. Chapman
Edited by Margaret Ford-Taylor

Grit

Greetings,

Today I would like to share some of my best advice on: GRIT! I know you are asking yourself "what did he just say?" About seven years ago I was checking my email when I read something online that talked about how important it is to have something called "grit." Someone had interviewed Professor Angela Duckworth about her findings on "grit" and how important it is to have or develop "grit" to get through difficult situations. The one word I personally took away from grit is (the cousin to grit) tenacity! The multi-millionaire author Seth Godin describes tenacity as *"using new data to make new decisions to find new pathways to find new ways to achieve a goal when the old ways didn't work."* Because of tenacity I can better understand grit and how it can be very beneficial to succeed in school and in life. The story behind how and why you're holding this book in your hand comes from me being *"gritty."*

In 2010 my God-daughter Mariah Weaver, was graduating from high school and I had a great idea for a graduation gift. That first idea did not work but it led me to developing the two books I currently have in the market place: *"My Best Advice Letters To Our Teenage Daughters* and *My Best Advice Letters To our Teenage Sons."* In short, I was determined and passionate about completing this book project and that is technically what Duckworth, is calling grit; *"a **combination** of **passion** and **perseverance** for a singularly important goal."* It took 22 months for me to complete the first book project. Imagine how people who loved me were looking at me over the course of those *gritty* 22 months. So, my best advice is when you find something that you desperately want to see done, **GO AND DO IT!** Take those <u>necessary small steps</u> and go for it! Do not let anyone or anything deter you because when you can <u>combine passion with perseverance</u>, the sky will become the limit. A wise man once said; *"the fastest way to kill a big dream/idea is to tell a small-minded/negative person."*

My suggestion is to write down your goals/dreams and read them every day. EVERDAY! No one can stop you with that never, never quit attitude of **TENACITY** and **GRIT!**

Have a great day!

Day 25 Journal

_____

_____

_____

_____

_____

_____

_____

_____

_____

_____

EMPOWERMENT DAY 26

By Anonymous
Edited by Margaret Ford-Taylor

Sex vs. abstinence

Greetings,

I recommend abstinence. So, first, let's start this discussion with the acknowledgement that the desire for sex is natural and normal. As a matter of fact, science states that the only physical desire stronger than the sexual urge is hunger. Every animal experiences these urgings, dogs, cats, rats, elephants, rabbits, lions, tigers and on and on and on. ALL animals have the urge to have sex. This urge, this feeling, allows each species to procreate. It does not require conscious thought, consideration or deliberation. After a certain age, sexual urges appear whether we want them to or not. In males, they appear as a physical phenomenon, often whether you want them to or not. It may or may not have anything to do with love. Sex can be an important part of a loving adult marriage relationship but should never be the most important or of singular consideration. When satisfying a sexual urge is a reason unto itself the act may be compared to urinating or having a bowel movement.

Both will relieve you temporarily but certainly have no relationship to any significant emotional experience. Too often, this genital reaction to the opposite sex encourages males and females alike to confuse it with that precious gift called love. What you will hopefully discover in your life time is that true love does many things but one thing it never does is promote action without serious thought. Too often what is being experienced is, simply, a very, very strong physical manifestation. Period. This is where human males should part from other male species. A key word here is "should". Unlike males of other species, the human male has the ability to reason, to think, to decide if succumbing to the sexual urge is a wise thing to do at this particular time.

There are too many critical considerations to have sex without the afore mentioned serious thought, among them are disease, potential pregnancy, respect for yourself, respect for the potential partner, your ability to rise above pure animal instinct and control yourself and your life. This is not easy. If we are hungry, it's hard to turn down junk food. Try to avoid becoming hungry for **sexual junk food**. Again, this is not easy. It takes discipline. It takes you making the decision to control your actions and your life. Sex is first of all physical. So, here are just a few tips. Make physical exercise a dominant part of your life. **Choose a sport. Run.**

Walk. Exercise. Hard. Also remember that even though sex is physical, *it is your ability to reason and think that is going to separate you from other male species.* So protect and expand your mind. For example, what has been determined to be the ten greatest books ever written? Find out. Read and study them. This action will take you right through your teen age years. Select a hobby that requires you to create something. Plan to do something for someone else once a week. Avoid scenes and scenarios where sex is the dominant factor. And speaking of the purely physical, frequent cold showers are a must. If abstinence is a serious consideration, you must have a plan and you must have self-discipline. Having said all of this, none of the advice given will stop you from wanting to have sex. Know that this is okay and natural. It's not how you feel that counts but, rather, what you do. It's up to you to use your brain and redirect those urgings to your benefit. And for the third time, it will not be easy—just smart. Sex can be a wonderful, sharing, experience between two thinking, caring, responsible adults. However, the first step toward obtaining that adulthood is recognizing and admitting to yourself that, if you are a teenager, you are still a child. **Having sex should be an adult/marriage undertaking.**

Have a great day!

Day 26 Journal

_____

_____

_____

_____

_____

_____

_____

_____

Empowerment Day 27

By Alonzo Qunnie
Edited by Margaret Ford-Taylor

Peer-Pressure

Greetings,

Peer-pressure can lead to experiencing some of the worse times in your life. Now I'm not saying that peer pressure is all bad, I'm just saying that good peer pressure and bad peer pressure are two totally different experiences. Bad peer pressure means negative, and on the flip side; good peer-pressure means positive. No one was meant or created to be alone in this world. Our society is basically set as a social environment. From birth, we're raised around family and friends. Normally these people are supposed to be people who we love and trust, people who we grow to love and respect because that's how we are groomed to believe. But what happens when we step outside of that comfort zone and start to attend schools, religious functions and events where other kids our age attend? What happens when all of a sudden, your clothes start looking out of place, girls start looking extra special to you and the things you are loyal to and respectful of growing up start getting put to the test by newly found feelings and circumstances? What happens and why? What is it that makes you feel different now? Have you ever asked yourself these questions? The answer is simple. It's called peer-pressure which means you are influenced by other people in your age group to act a certain way.

My name is Alonzo, and I was born in 1977. I'm the second oldest of five. My mother is a single parent and the more her family grew, the deeper times became harder for us. My first initiation came in the first grade with the pledge of allegiance to the flag. A pledge I can recite to this day. One of the reasons I am telling you a little bit about my life is because I want you to get an idea of how *early* peer-pressure can enter your life without you even noticing it. Being in school and growing up with all of the kids I knew back then was some of the most impressionable years of my life. As a kid I remember playing games like hide and go seek, doctor, and tag. These games were mainly decided by who ever made it to the playground first. At that age I never would have believed that those childhood experiences would ultimately open up to the life of peer-pressure. But they did. <u>What the other kids did and thought mattered even at that young age</u>. I was raised to respect my elders and to play fair. My mother did whatever she could to make sure we always had what we needed and that we knew right from wrong. My next adventures started in junior high school.

Each generation has its own swagger to it. Back then we rocked Air Max, Nautica, Polo, Cross Colours, Tommy Hilfiger, Levi's, and Starter Coats. We listened to Rap & R&B; rappers like Scarface, N.W.A, and the Ghetto Boyz had the airwaves on lock. All my friends were experiencing some form of peer-pressure whether it was smoking weed or having sex, the pressure to fit in was heavy. Money somehow was creeping its head into the picture too. Without a couple of dollars in our pockets, having fun or what we believed at the time was having fun; was impossible. Without money you didn't fit in, and if you didn't fit in, then that meant that you didn't have any influence. In my neighborhood, most men rarely maintained meaningful relationships with their children and their mothers. I was raised around a lot of single parents. Our mothers could only do what they thought was right and if a mother had more than one child in her care she would eventually be spread thin and dudes like me would obviously be forced to work for what we wanted, at a very young age. Jobs at local grocery stores, cutting lawns and running errands for the elderly usually were a quick way to earn a buck. However, in my neighborhood, selling drugs was quicker. Peer-pressure had its way with me for years. My high school years were the worse. That life-style that I chose to start living would eventually end me up in juvenile detention for a year, only to become a high school dropout when I was released. By the time I turned 19 years old I had been in two major car accidents; several shoot-outs and had turned into a convicted felon at the same time. Today I write you this letter from a prison library. I'm serving a life sentence for being loyal to the so-called street code. I didn't take the stand against some dudes I grew up with in a crime I literally had nothing to do with. Running around the street, representing my hood, (the Southside of Cleveland, Ohio) back then made feel like I was a part of something special, something different. What I failed to realize was the fact that I was slipping from my natural positive way of thinking to a negative way of thinking. Not knowing is not an excuse when it comes to the system. They have one job and that job is to protect the public from criminal's no matter if it was a mistake or not.

See, we are all born innocent. Everything we do is either taught to us or we pick it up or we learn it from somebody around us. Positive peer-pressure and negative peer-pressure are forms of either good guidance or bad guidance. The whole key is for **YOU** to become the deciding factor. It all boils down to the choices **YOU** make. From now on I want you to try to act on all positive thoughts that come to mind, and **I want you to build the voice inside of you to not allow yourself to just go for anything**.

Make your intentions as pure as you can because the intentions from the beginning will usually be the end results just as the end result will usually be the intention from the beginning.

There is a three-step process to straight power. **Think. Speak. Do. Think** about it. **Speak** on it. **Do** it. Give yourself that chance in this game of life and I guarantee success. Don't allow peer-pressure to ruin years of your life the way I did. Make peer-pressure work for you by using your God given positive voice and start acting on your positive thoughts. It could save the lives of others as well as your own. Stay thorough and be on your best behavior. I do not know everything, but I can say this: **God made you in the image of Himself. It was written.**

You are already destined for greatness and can't nobody take away from you but you. **YOU ARE THE FUTURE**...Don't allow peer-pressure to run you anymore. It's time for you to run it. Positively speaking!

Have a great day!

Day 27 Journal

Empowerment Day 28

By David Colin
Edited by Margaret Ford-Taylor

Entrepreneurship

Greetings,

As a kid I always had envisioned becoming an entrepreneur. I remember spending a few summers in Cleveland, Ohio working with my grandfather at his bar. He taught me a lot about business, how to act like an owner and how to treat people with respect. These words of wisdom have stuck with me to this day and now I am the co-owner of **Razor Sharp Kutz of Elk Grove, California & founder of Cali Barber**. Cutting hair has always been a passion of mine since middle school. I recognized early how something as simple as a haircut can change one's physical and mental appearance. We all have a calling in life. I believe if you do what you love then your calling will find YOU. The art of barbering is so much more than a haircut and a shave. It's a service. It's about a professional skill. I am committed to providing exceptional personal care to my clients of all ages at Razor Sharp Kutz precision is everything with more than 15 years of experience. It took more than a decade for me to realize the job I thought would be my career didn't exist. I had to learn to create the work I loved. No one can decide what that is for you except you. You must explore who you are, what you like, how you live, what you know, and what energizes you, even when you're tired. Conscious decisions about managing money are critical if you intend to become an entrepreneur. You are responsible for the success of your own business. You may need a business partner or investor. Professional training and certification, networking events, trade shows, and prospering mentors will be the best tools and resources to help you and your business grow. You will need a support system to help you with advice, encouragement, and leadership. Know the difference between selling and serving. Always think about delivering the best product and the most courteous, friendly service. Together, these will add value for your business. Who are you? These are the traits, good and bad, of entrepreneurs. You're a natural leader, not a follower. You are a creative thinker. You're extremely perceptive, able to see the big picture. You are self-motivated. You can be impatient, stubborn, deaf to the ideas of other people, and territorial. What do you like? You are competitive. You enjoy a challenge and the thrill of the game. You are generally at ease with people.

You tend to handle stress better than most people. You are self-confident. You have a positive self-image. You take risks. You like to be in charge. How do you live? You make rigorous demands of yourself and others. You work hard. You play hard. You are willing to make sacrifices for what you want. What do you know? You know that there is always a better way to do things. What energizes you? Self-satisfaction drives your commitment. You take pride in doing your best. In the beginning, you will have to advertise your business and yourself through social media, word-of-mouth, emails, blogs, and this will let your clients, fans, and followers know you are a serious entrepreneur.

After all, you have to be confident in who you are and what you do. I have taken advantage of local television news interviews featuring new neighborhood businesses and industry events such as hosting barber training with master barbers and competing in "barber battles" and barbering contests. You have to stay close and well-connected to the pulse of whatever business you choose. This is how you become an expert in your chosen professional business venture.

Read about planning and growing a business: *Become Your Own Boss In 12 Months* by Melinda Emerson, *Do You* by Russell Simmons, *The Audacity of Hope* by Barack Obama, *The Brand Within* by Daymond John, and *Think and Grow Rich* by Napoleon Hill.

Do yourself a favor and talk to entrepreneurs who are doing what you dream of doing as your life's work. My grandfather planted a seed many years ago in a small, neighborhood bar in Cleveland, Ohio by telling me and showing me what it means to transform the tenacity of a stubborn teenager into the success of an entrepreneur.

Have a great day!

Day 28 Journal

_____

_____

_____

_____

_____

_____

_____

_____

_____

_____

Empowerment Day 29

By Kevin Willingham
Edited by Margaret Ford-Taylor

Fatherhood

Greetings,

Every man's entrance to fatherhood will be different, some by choice others by circumstance. A good percentage of successful men were fortunate to have a father figure in their life's. In the many peaks and valleys of life, it is essentials that young men have a mentor to turn to. And most of all have a relationship with your spiritual father. Having a relationship with your Heavenly Father is extremely important. There will come a time in your life when you'll have to lean on the Spiritual lesson learned at YOUR Spiritual home of worship. Being active with your Spiritual family is nothing but a bonus. This is where valuable lessons will be taught from the elders you share time with. So, if you're not involved with a Spiritual Family I strongly recommend doing so.

Entering fatherhood by circumstance. Most of the time this happens between two people who are just children them self's.

Maybe no one took the time to have a discussion with them about having sex. Making the choice to have sex at a young age put your future in danger. Don't be afraid to talk with your father, big brother, uncle or that person you trust. Becoming a father at a young age can change your future tremendously. Some young men are fortunate to have that person of trust in their life. Most of the time it's a father, or an uncle, or someone who see's something special in you and be willing to take the time to share some life experiences with you that will help you alone the way in your life. If your smart enough to listen, you'll avoid a lot of setbacks in life and be shown how to evaluate and make good choices.

Know that you are loved and an important part of one's life. Know that you can always lean on your spiritual father when needed. *Know that* you can show accountability and responsibility and live respectful. Know that you are a leader and not a follower. Know that there will come a day when you'll be the father or that person who is look to for love and direction.

Have a great day!

Day 29 Journal

EMPOWERMENT DAY 30

By Reggie Thompson
Edited by Margaret Ford-Taylor

Education

Greetings,

The one thing that is more expensive: the lack of an education. There are a number of degrees of education, well educated, uneducated, under–educated. there are also those that are considered over educated. And then there are those who are victims of the no child left behind act, which has been an abject failure (in my opinion). Consequently, you have the responsibility of securing the best education that is available to you, in an effort to realize your own potential. Surely, you've been told these things since you began school. As a result of your experiences with your school system, be it rural, municipal or private along with charter you may have come away with different perceptions of what education affords you. Ideally and primarily there should be critical thinking skills, the ability to socially interact, conflict resolution and the basics of Math, English, History and the Sciences.

The law dictates that you must attend school, pride should mandate that you perform at your highest level as it becomes the foundation for all that is to come. Your employment and thereby your ability to provide for yourself is in direct correlation as to how well you successfully complete your education. In this highly technological atmosphere education is crucial to your future. Check with those you consider doing well and take a survey of their educational accomplishments you should find that those who have acquired post high-school education have more success. Education is the barometer by which we determine qualifications in this society, and there are no longer any reasons why one should be disqualified. Just as a well-educated person is afforded greater possibilities for achievement, the lack of an education becomes a hindrance to realizing your full and complete potential. Fortunately, today the choice is completely yours. I compel you young man to accept all the education that is offered to you, for in doing so you provide yourself with something that can never be taken from you. Jobs come and go, relationships may change, change is a way of life, but education is forever and never ending, thereby making it **one of the most valuable commodities you will ever acquire**. As a result of having lived beyond my teen years I find it my responsibility to promote the importance of education, if only one of you heeds this call to endure to best of your ability

142

I will have given back a small portion of what has been given to me.

The fact that you are reading this book gives me hope and assures me this call to educate yourselves have/will not fall upon deaf ears. **Learn so that you may earn respect, live so that you may give to someone who needs.** I thank you for your time and I wish you well in your endeavors.

Have a great day!

Day 30 Journal

Empowerment Day 31

By William (Bill) Johnson
Edited by Margaret Ford-Taylor

Healthy Competition

Greetings,

Today I want to discuss Healthy Competition, Winston Churchill said "success is never fatal. Failure is never final" It is most unfortunate that so much is made of success in sports and life without talking about what it took to get there. Nor is a great deal made of failure and how it can lead to success. For a long time, the opening statement for the wide world of sports was *"the thrill of victory, and the agony of defeat."* However most successful athletes and individuals have only got there once they knew how to accept and learn from failure. Michael Jordan was cut from his high school basketball team and did not win a championship on his first try. Nor did Lebron James win a championship during his first few years as a cavalier. However, what drove them both was *their will to compete and learning from their failures to reach the ultimate goal in sport.* It took lots of hard work, practice and mental and physical training. Allen Iverson, a popular and truly gifted athlete, never won a championship. Yet he was still one of basketball's greatest competitors.

145

Lebron almost carried the cavaliers to a championship in 2016 through force of will alone. Yet it was the lessons learned from that defeat which fueled his desire to succeed that brought the first championship to Cleveland in over fifty years. The Chicago cubs defeated my beloved Indians in a seven game classic world series. Neither team's city had experienced a baseball championship in recent history (Chicago over one hundred years, and Cleveland over seventy). Yet both teams gave it their all. Finally, Sergio Garcia won the masters golf tournament this year, after over a decade of not winning this particular tournament.

Healthy competition is important in every area of your life especially is school. While you may not be competing during your twelve years of education, you will compete with other students worldwide for scholarships during the last four years of high school. Sports can help you succeed in school and in life whether you become a professional or not. However, what happens if you don't succeed, when you fall flat on your face. Here ae some people who continued and succeeded against all odds. The light bulb was developed by Thomas Edison, after he failed over nine hundred times. The Wright Brothers were initially trying to build a helicopter not an airplane.

Abraham Lincoln lost just about every election except two, the last was for president of the United States of America. Numerous African American inventors had to overcome tremendous opposition just to receive patents for their products and services. But they prevailed. Healthy competition, however, does not have to be combative. It can be fun without being violent or combative. It should not lead to physical confrontations. Nor should it be so important that someone tries to injure an opponent on purpose. That is not competitive, no matter the sport. **Competition should always remain healthy** and free from the insanity. Trash talking is okay as long as it does not get personal. It is said the journey of a thousand miles begins with one step. The key word is journey. All steps will not be successful. **However, it is the continual striving for success in the face of failure that leads to victory in all aspects of life.** It is not always about winning, but how you play/live that counts.

Have a great day!

Day 31 Journal

"Goals that are not written down are just wishes."

-Anonymous

PART TWO

ALL ABOUT GOALS

STOP!

Please read this important information on goal setting

First, let's ask ourselves the question, what are goals? According to Webster's dictionary, a goal is "something that you are trying to do or achieve." Do you want to succeed in your studies, in athletics, or in any of the many other areas of your life? Of course, you do!

Goal setting is a major key. The President of the United States does it. CEO's of large corporations do it. Elementary, Middle and High School principals do it. Most people who are successful in life practice goal setting. Why? The number one reason why you should set goals is because goals serve as a blue print or road map to where you want to go as a teen or as an adult. Just as there are maps to navigate one's traveling, your goals sheets (on the following pages) will serve the same purpose. The number two reason why you should set goals is so that you can be specific and clear about where you are going. Once you begin your goal setting program, watch out for setbacks. One of the principle ingredients to have in place to help avoid setbacks is **accountability**. Nothing in this world is 100%.

However, if you want to avoid simple pit falls and unnecessary road blocks, **find a partner, someone you can be accountable to.** Your *"accountability partner"* can be a parent, a teacher, a coach, a mentor or any other adult that you trust and who you know wants to see you succeed. Make a date with your accountability partner and discuss with them how you plan to proceed and ask for their suggestions, comments and concerns. Take notes at each meeting. Have them sign off on your beginning plan. Set up a schedule to meet with your partner for thirty minutes each week to discuss your progress.

It will be their job to sign off on the bottom of your Goals Sheet each marking period, agreeing that you will meet your goals for that particular marking period. When the going gets tough, and you get discouraged, tired, lazy TALK TO YOUR ACCOUNTABILITY PARTNER. Once you have had your initial meeting with your accountability partner decide specifically what it is you want to accomplish. Then plan and take one small step at a time to make it happen. Each step leads you to the next step and you continue the process until you are at the top or at least where you want to go.

The goals sections found in this book have been designed to assist you each marking period in establishing goals and then, by taking one small step at a time, achieving them. In setting your goals, try not to generalize. For example, you might say, "I want better grades next marking period." A stronger, more helpful goal to set would be, *"I plan to move from a "D" to a "B" by the end of the marking period."* Instead of saying, "I plan to lose some weight by the end of the marking period," say **"I will lose 10 lbs. by the end of the marking period."** Remember, small steps are better.

Working with your accountability partner and using the goals sheets found in this book, each marking period you will decide exactly what it is you want to achieve and the steps you plan to take to succeed. Remember, small changes can make a big difference and there's no such thing as failure. I like to call them second chances and sometimes we can all use a second chance. So, don't beat yourself up if you just "come close." You still have the next marking period to improve. **SO, STICK TO IT! The victory will be sweet.** There's an old tried and true adage that works here. "If at first you don't succeed, try, try again." Challenge yourself to do better. You don't have to push yourself to the limit all the time, but you should want to move closer to your goals each marking period. One size does not fit all. You are you so make your goals with that in mind. Your ATTITUDE will play a big part in whether you win or lose. A quote that I personally love is, *"It is the attitude that you have toward yourself that will determine your attitude toward your world."* Now, every small step you take, large or small, **CELEBRATE!** Do something nice for yourself and look forward to achieving your next goal. Most importantly, **HAVE FUN!** SO, **ON YOUR MARK, GET SET, GO!** From the mouth of Zig Ziglar, *"SEE YOU AT THE TOP!"*

FIRST SCHOOL YEAR
20___-20_____

FIRST MARKING PERIOD

GOAL #1_____

_____

STEP #3_____

_____

STEP #2_____

_____

STEP #1_____

_____

GOAL #2_____

_____

STEP #3_____

_____

STEP #2_____

_____

STEP #1_____

Accountability Partner Signature:_____

SECOND MARKING PERIOD

GOAL #1_____

_____

STEP #3_____

_____

STEP #2_____

_____

STEP #1_____

_____

GOAL #2_____

_____

STEP #3_____

_____

STEP #2_____

_____

STEP #1_____

Accountability Partner Signature:_____

THIRD MARKING PERIOD

GOAL #1_____

_____

STEP #3_____

_____

STEP #2_____

_____

STEP #1_____

_____

GOAL #2_____

_____

STEP #3_____

_____

STEP #2_____

_____

STEP #1_____

Accountability Partner Signature:_____

FOURTH MARKING PERIOD

GOAL #1_____

_____

STEP #3_____

_____

STEP #2_____

_____

STEP #1_____

_____

GOAL #2_____

_____

STEP #3_____

_____

STEP #2_____

_____

STEP #1_____

Accountability Partner Signature:_____

SECOND SCHOOL YEAR
20___-20_____

FIRST MARKING PERIOD

GOAL #1_____

_____

STEP #3_____

_____

STEP #2_____

_____

STEP #1_____

_____

GOAL #2_____

_____

STEP #3_____

_____

STEP #2_____

_____

STEP #1_____

Accountability Partner Signature:_____

SECOND MARKING PERIOD

GOAL #1_____

_____

STEP #3_____

_____

STEP #2_____

_____

STEP #1_____

_____

GOAL #2_____

_____

STEP #3_____

_____

STEP #2_____

_____

STEP #1_____

_____

Accountability Partner Signature:_____

THIRD MARKING PERIOD

GOAL #1_____

_____

STEP #3_____

_____

STEP #2_____

_____

STEP #1_____

_____

GOAL #2_____

_____

STEP #3_____

_____

STEP #2_____

_____

STEP #1_____

_____

Accountability Partner Signature:_____

FOURTH MARKING PERIOD

GOAL #1_____

_____

STEP #3_____

_____

STEP #2_____

_____

STEP #1_____

_____

GOAL #2_____

_____

STEP #3_____

_____

STEP #2_____

_____

STEP #1_____

_____

Accountability Partner Signature:_____

THIRD SCHOOL YEAR
20___-20_____

FIRST MARKING PERIOD

GOAL #1_____

_____

STEP #3_____

_____

STEP #2_____

_____

STEP #1_____

_____

GOAL #2_____

_____

STEP #3_____

_____

STEP #2_____

_____

STEP #1_____

Accountability Partner Signature:_____

SECOND MARKING PERIOD

GOAL #1_____

_____

STEP #3_____

_____

STEP #2_____

_____

STEP #1_____

_____

GOAL #2_____

_____

STEP #3_____

_____

STEP #2_____

_____

STEP #1_____

Accountability Partner Signature:_____

THIRD MARKING PERIOD

GOAL #1_____

_____

STEP #3_____

_____

STEP #2_____

_____

STEP #1_____

_____

GOAL #2_____

_____

STEP #3_____

_____

STEP #2_____

_____

STEP #1_____

Accountability Partner Signature:_____

FOURTH MARKING PERIOD

GOAL #1_____

_____

STEP #3_____

_____

STEP #2_____

_____

STEP #1_____

_____

GOAL #2_____

_____

STEP #3_____

_____

STEP #2_____

_____

STEP #1_____

Accountability Partner Signature:_____

Order & Contact Information

ORDER NOW!
Amazon.Com/BluZipper Books

Email
bluzipper@gmail.com

SOCIAL MEDIA
All Social Media@/BluZipper Media

ABOUT THE EDITOR

Margaret Ford-Taylor is a nationally acclaimed writer, director, actress and arts administrator. Among many critically recognized acting awards and commendations, she received her first Emmy nomination for her performance in the public television production, "American Women: Echoes and Dreams." Her last film appearance was as Aunt Edy in Denzel Washington's Antwon Fisher.

Author of more than 40 critically acknowledged and nationally produced stage works, Miss Ford-Taylor's second Emmy nomination was as the writer of the ABC television documentary, "The Second Reconstruction."

She was affiliated with the world-renown Karamu Performing Arts Center of Cleveland, Ohio for more than 30 years, serving as its Executive Director for ten.

She has taught on the faculties of Kent State University and Akron University, retiring from the Dramatic Arts Faculty of Cleveland State University in 2008. As a teacher and mentor many of her students are recognized among the list of noted professionals in the performing arts field and other industries.

About The Co-Author

As far back as I can remember I have been interested in entrepreneurship. It all started when I was a paper boy with the Cleveland Press News-Paper. At 11 years of age I won a contest for signing up new customers. After a long afternoon of delivering papers I was approached by some guys I knew from my neighborhood. They said "Hey, paper boy, you want to make some real money, you need to come hang with us" All the while they were laughing. A short time after that, I join their gang on the Eastside of Cleveland and begin my introduction to experimenting with drugs and alcohol. I didn't realize it then but I had just enrolled into "side-walk University" to major in *"street-sense."* I am amazed at how far *"street sense"* can take you...Unfortunately, that's exactly where it will also leave you. That is also where I begin a career of always trying to gain an upper hand on any and every situation. After a few years with that bunch I wanted out. I thought I had escaped with only the small scar under my bottom lip where I received stitches from being hit and kicked because I made a decision to leave a life of negativity and begin living more positively. Unfortunately, the beginning stages of alcohol and drug abuse along with an extreme case of emotional immaturity were present as well.

172

Hence, there were a number of detours. Once, during one detour, I was over 800 miles away from home, addicted, homeless twice, with the possibility of federal prison looming over my head; that was coupled with strong feelings of guilt, shame, and remorse. I begin to realize that I had just squandered one of the most precious years of my life...**My YOUTH.** As an adult I tried on several occasion to gain those years back, but to no avail and that was a troubling reality that I had to accept. Somehow, I eventually managed to navigate my way through high school, graduating on the merit roll and with perfect attendance. I always had a strong thirst for knowledge. So I'm not surprised that today I work around educators, who I BELIEVE are some of the brightest and talented in their field (Mary M. Bethune School 2011-2012). But back then, I was still clue less. One day, through divine intervention, I decided I had had enough and I made up my mind to throw in the towel. I was FORTUNATE. With some good counseling and willing workers, I BEGAN the journey of rebuilding my life mentally, physically, emotionally, and spiritually all *"one day at a time."*

However, when I juxtapose to where I am today it's no comparison. I am extremely grateful.

Currently, I reside in University Circle in the great *"comeback"* City, Cleveland, Ohio. In January 2012 the notable Forbes Magazine voted University Circle as one of the 10-prettiest neighborhoods In America.

Presently, I work not far from where I live at a Pre-K-8 school where I am a Paraprofessional (a really cool name for an assistant teacher). I work with children with special needs. My current assignment is a one-on-one with an 11-year-old student name Trevon who has autism. (Relax everyone. His parents approved of me using his name). Trevon doesn't communicate very well. He repeats everything. It's called **"echolalia."** Trevon is special to me. In his own way, he's taught me so much. So, I pause at this time in my life to give a brief shout out to my little buddy. Trevon has a gentle spirit. He is extremely funny, a sharp dresser in and out of school uniform and a lover of all kinds of music, especially the BLUES, and an all-around joy to work with.

With no hesitation I will say working with Trevon has been one of the highlights and best experiences of my ENTIRE adult working career.

Let me pause to say, if you have special needs students in your life; treat them with love, respect, and genuine kindness. YOU'LL be the winner and God will bless your life for that. Finally, my hope is that this book will inspire someone to follow their dreams and never let them die. I close with one of my favorite sayings from the scriptures, *"the race is not given to the swift nor to the strong but to those who endure to...THE END!"*

ACKNOWLEDGEMENTS

First and foremost, I MUST thank God for His
"AMAZING GRACE!"

-Your Son, Michael Kenneth Chapman!

To Mom and Willie: Thanks for the Thursday steak dinners–and I do mean every Thursday, [unless my *"big brother"* George or my first-cousin Tiffany Moore beat me to it] smile.   -Your Son, Michael!

To my immediate family: My Aunt Gloria Moore, my *big brother* George D. Chapman, my two older sisters Debra M. Chapman and Nadine M. Chapman, all my 1st, 2nd, 3rd, and 4th, cousins and all my nieces and nephews. Thank you all for listening to me **EVERY** Thanksgiving about every wild and crazy idea I have ever brought to the dinner table, most importantly, thank you all for not laughing at me...Well, at least not in my face–thank you guys and I Love you all!   -Michael!

To Miss Margaret Ford-Taylor: You are more than just a great editor, writer, actress and acting coach you are truly a great friend...You are an author's dream and your gift will be a blessing to many young women around the world...Thanks for your support, wisdom and expertise...May God continue to bless your life.   -Michael!

To my man-of-God Dr. R. A. Vernon and first lady, Lady Vernon: I thank you both for speaking into my life since April 11, 2004 (Easter Sunday) and for always *"N-COURAGING"* me to go to the next level in ALL areas of my life.   -Brother Chapman

To my son, Quameen *"Q"* Vernon: You will be a strong leader in your chosen field and I will continue to tell you that until I see it manifested. You have charisma and people like you for you. Always follow your heart, but make sure you finish your master's program! God bless you! -   Love always, Dad!

To my beautiful God–daughter, Mariah *"Precious"* Weaver: God has an AWESOME plan for your life and I will live to see it come to pass. I truly appreciate you being in my life...With all my heart I love you very much! By the way, have you read your *"One-Year-Bible"* today?

-Love always, Your God-Father!

To the 31-letter writers: This book would have ALL blank pages had it not been for you **ALL**. May God continue to bless *ALL* of you and your families!

-Michael K. Chapman

Made in the USA
Columbia, SC
01 September 2019